Classic Irish Recipes

Georgina Campbell
Illustrated by Marlene Ekman

Sterling Publishing Co., Inc.   New York

Library of Congress Cataloging-in-Publication Data

Campbell, Georgina.
    Classic Irish recipes / Georgina Campbell ; illustrations by
Marlene Ekman.
        p.   cm.
    This book is excerpted from Good Food from Ireland, originally
published in Great Britain by Grafton Books.
    Includes index.
    ISBN 0-8069-8444-9
    1. Cookery, Irish.   I. Title.
TX717.5.C36   1992
641.59415 — dc20   91-43520
                                                                   CIP

To my parents, who taught me the love of good food: my
mother, who instilled in me the importance of top-quality
ingredients and allowed me to practice in her kitchen from an
early age, and my father, who provided many of those ingredients himself and has always been wonderfully appreciative of
every meal.

10   9   8   7   6   5   4   3   2   1

Published in 1992 by Sterling Publishing Company, Inc.
387 Park Avenue South, New York, N.Y. 10016
Editorial arrangement © 1992 by Sterling Publishing Company
This book is excerpted from *Good Food from Ireland*
Originally published in Great Britain by Grafton Books
a division of HarperCollins*Publishers*
© 1991 by Georgina Campbell
Distributed in Canada by Sterling Publishing
% Canadian Manda Group, P.O. Box 920, Station U
Toronto, Ontario, Canada M8Z 5P9
Manufactured in the United States of America

Sterling ISBN 0-8069-8444-9

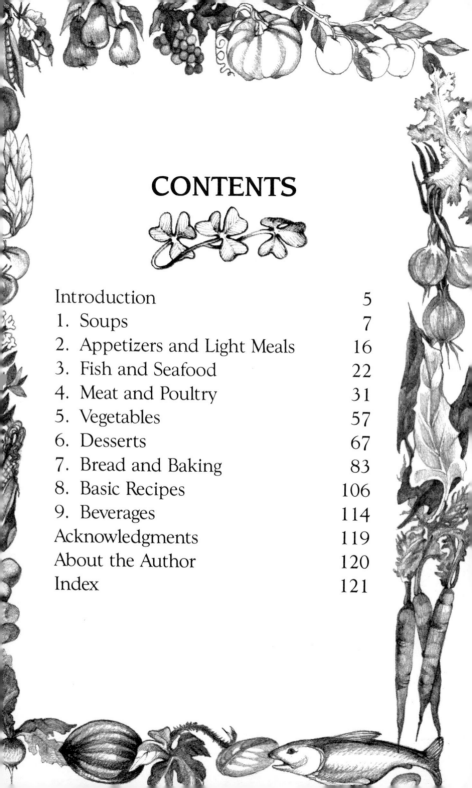

CONTENTS

◆ Introduction ◆

Galway oysters, Limerick ham, Atlantic salmon, Dublin Bay prawns, Wexford mussels — all wonderful Irish produce, renowned for its freshness and quality, yet the fickleness of fashion kept the traditional dishes based on these native foods out of favor for many years. Recently, however, the tide of fashion has turned, and the old recipes that have been handed down through the generations are again highly prized for their wonderful wholesomeness and simplicity. All the great classics are back — Cockle and Mussel Chowder, Dublin Coddle, Cruibins, Irish Stew, Corned Beef with Dumplings and Cabbage, Colcannon, Champ, Boxty, Soda Bread and Barm Brack — and here they are, just as they've been handed down from one hospitable Irish cook to the next.

Irish hospitality may be legendary, but is no myth. According to the ancient Brehon Laws, which date back to the fifth century A.D., people in higher stations were obliged to entertain guests "without asking any questions." In the eighteenth century, a particularly happy period in Irish history, and an age when keeping a journal was *de rigueur*, travelers reported on the range and quality of Irish produce set before guests with an enthusiasm that occasionally bordered on incredulity. One extraordinary story concerned a housewarming party at which the dining room was unfinished on the day of the event and two guests who fell asleep in their chairs actually got their heads stuck to the newly plastered walls!

The hearth was a particularly important factor in the development of Irish cooking. Turf and wood, which both burn easily in a fireplace at ground level, were the most common fuels until relatively recently, and all the cooking was done in a variety of utensils that were hung or set on a trivet over the fire — a fact that had great bearing on the character of traditional dishes. The main utensil was the cast-iron three-legged pot (origin of the expression "pot luck"), which varied from small one-gallon pots to enormous ones holding 20 gallons or more, used for heating water. Baking and roasting were done in flat-bottomed three-legged "pot-ovens" or "bastables," one used exclusively for breadmaking, which were designed to take hot turves c⁀ peat on the lid to give all-around heat. Flat-bottomed skillets and frying pans were set on a trivet, as were small long-handled pans and "mullers," which were used for heating liquids and drinks. Griddles were kept in several sizes for making scones, potato bread, and so on, and spit-roasting was also quite common. About 250 years ago iron ranges began to appear in the big houses of the gentry, and then gradually down through prosperous farmhouses and so on, but the three-legged pot was still very much in use early this century.

Sadly, the nineteenth century is remembered mainly for the needless cycle of poverty and starvation that led inexorably to the ultimate tragedy of the Great Famine. Understandably, memories of those times have died hard and have undoubtedly influenced the way in which Irish people regard their culinary heritage. It is really only in the last decade, when visitors to this wonderfully productive island have recognized and highlighted the great benefits that are so easily taken for granted, that the Irish people have begun to reassess traditional Irish food.

Two individuals stand head and shoulders above the crowd as champions of Irish food. The late Theodora FitzGibbon, *Irish Times* cookery columnist and author of countless books, wrote *A Taste of Ireland*, the first of the current generation of books on traditional Irish food, in 1968, a good 20 years before it was fashionable to do so. She was always consistent in her support of good traditional and country cooking. So has Myrtle Allen, founder with her husband, Ivan, of what is now frequently referred to as "the Ballymaloe dynasty" — the internationally acclaimed Ballymaloe House Hotel and its associated businesses. Darina Allen's cookery school, Wendy Allen's kitchen shop and Fern Allen's restaurant in the Crawford Gallery in Cork, Ireland, owe a great debt to Myrtle Allen for her tremendous instinct for good, simple food, and her determination to accept nothing but the best. Thanks to the efforts of people like these, the chances of getting superb results are increasing all the time. See for yourself — try out some of these classic Irish recipes in your own kitchen.

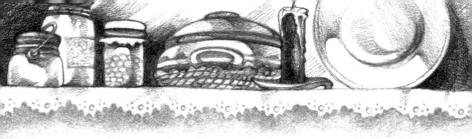

1. Soups

Traditional Irish soups are simple and filling, based on ingredients that have always been inexpensive and easily available, especially vegetables such as onions, leeks, carrots, turnips, potatoes, garlic and nettles. Potatoes are relatively new, having been cultivated in Ireland only since the seventeenth century, but native plants such as leeks, garlic and nettles go back a great deal further. The word "pottage," an early form of soup, is said to derive from the Latin *porrus* for leek, and garlic was important enough to have a day named after it — Garlick Sunday was the first Sunday in August, after which, in the eighteenth and nineteenth centuries, the previous season's potatoes were relegated to feeding the pigs and oatmeal became the staple food until the new crop came in. Nettles provided a free and tasty ingredient for soups in spring, and — as they are rich in vitamins and minerals, and said to cleanse the blood — they were also taken as a medicinal herbal tea on three consecutive days beginning on May Day.

Small pieces of chicken, meat, fish or shellfish were included in

soups when they were available and, as the object was to make soups as filling and nourishing as possible, the line between traditional soups and stews is often very fine — some of the soups here need only some homemade bread to accompany them to become a complete meal.

To anyone unfamiliar with Ireland, soup, politics and religion might seem to have little in common, but during the famine they became inextricably entwined. First a famous French chef from the London Reform Club, Alexis Soyer, came to Dublin and established soup kitchens in an attempt to check starvation. All went remarkably well until he published his recipes, emphasizing how little meat was needed for some of his soups and none at all for others. These recipes caused what can only be described as an unholy row in the press — even the *Lancet* joined in, claiming that a diet of soup and one biscuit daily was not adequate to maintain life. The story ended sadly, with public resentment at such an hysterical level that the well-meaning Soyer had to leave Ireland secretly to escape being lynched.

Later, large Protestant landowners set up similar soup kitchens for the starving peasants, most of whom were Roman Catholics. The landowners were accused of using the distribution of soup as a proselytizing medium, so those who took the soup and changed their religion were called "soupers." Even to this day Protestants with Roman Catholic names are said to be descended from the "soupers." On a happier note, during the last war (known as "The Emergency" in the south of Ireland) women of the Dublin St. John's Ambulance Brigade ran a very successful soup kitchen, supplying thousands of substantial meals to expectant mothers, children and old people. Of course, medical opinion now endorses Soyer's approach, and the traditional recipes given here, however simple, are extremely nourishing and healthy.

⟶◆ *Beef Broth with Barley* ◆⟶

This traditional farmhouse soup has changed very little through the generations.

1–1½ pounds beef chuck blade steak or other stewing beef on the bone
2 large onions
3–4 carrots
1–2 white turnips
2–3 celery stalks
1 large or 2 medium leeks
¼ cup pearl barley
¼ cup split green peas
Sea salt and freshly ground black pepper
Freshly chopped parsley to garnish

First bone the meat and put the bones and half of one of the onions, roughly sliced, into a large pan. Cover with cold water, season and bring to the boil; skim if necessary, then let simmer covered for 1½– 2 hours or until needed. Meanwhile, trim any fat or gristle from the meat and cut it into small pieces. Peel and chop finely the remaining onions. Peel and chop the carrots and white turnips; chop the celery; and wash the leeks thoroughly and slice finely.

Drain the stock from the bones, add enough water to make 7 cups, and return it to the rinsed pan along with the meat, onions, barley and split peas. Season with salt and pepper, bring to the boil and skim if necessary. Reduce the heat, cover and let simmer for about half an hour. Add the rest of the vegetables and simmer gently for an hour or so, until the meat is tender. Check the seasoning, then serve in large bowls generously sprinkled with freshly chopped parsley.

Serves 6–8.

⟶ *Brotchán Foltchep* ◆⟶

This traditional leek and oatmeal soup is also known as Brotchán Roy. It combines three ingredients — leeks, oatmeal and milk — that were staple foods in Ireland for centuries. In country districts it is often adapted to make nettle soup in the spring, when the nettle tops are young and tender.

> 1 quart Chicken Stock (see page 107) and milk, mixed
> 2 rounded tablespoons medium McCann's Irish Oatmeal
> 6 large leeks
> 2 tablespoons butter
> Sea salt and freshly ground black pepper
> Pinch of ground mace
> 2 rounded tablespoons freshly chopped parsley
> Whipping cream and chopped parsley or chives to garnish
>   (optional)

Bring the stock and milk mixture to a boil over moderate heat and sprinkle in the oatmeal. Stir well to prevent lumps forming, then bring to a simmer. Meanwhile, trim the leeks, leaving most of the green part on, and cut them into rings about ¾ inch long. Wash thoroughly in cold water and drain well.

Melt the butter in a pan over gentle heat, add the leeks and cook until they soften slightly. Add the leeks to the simmering stock mixture. Season with salt, pepper and mace and simmer for 15–20 minutes more, or until the oatmeal is cooked. Add extra stock or milk if the soup is too thick. Stir in the chopped parsley and serve in warmed bowls, which can be decorated with a swirl of cream and some freshly chopped parsley or chives, if you like.

Serves 4–6.

→ *Cockle and Mussel Chowder* ←

Thanks to Molly Malone, cockles and mussels are probably the most famous foods connected with Dublin.

6 tablespoons butter
¾ cup all-purpose flour
About 6½ cups fish stock (see page 107)
About 1½ cups dry white wine
½ potato, finely chopped
2 stalks celery, chopped
1 handful freshly chopped parsley
1 level teaspoon freshly chopped dill
4 ounces shelled cockles (or use mussels, oysters,
    or additional mussels)
6 ounces shelled mussels
Sea salt and freshly ground black pepper
Heavy cream
Cooked cockles and mussels in their shells to garnish
    (optional)

Melt the butter in a large heavy-bottomed saucepan. Add the flour, blend well and cook gently for a minute or two. Gradually whisk in the fish stock, blending smoothly, and add most of the wine. Add the finely chopped potato, chopped celery, herbs, cockles and mussels. Cook for 8–10 minutes, until the vegetables are tender, season to taste, then stir in enough cream to correct the consistency and flavor. Cook for a couple of minutes, adjust the flavor if necessary by adding the remaining wine or some milk to sharpen or dilute the soup. Then serve garnished with a few cooked cockles and mussels in their shells.

Serves 6–7.

—◆ *Kidney and Bacon Soup* ◆—

This updated variation on a continental classic is another of Georgina O'Sullivan's creations from The Meat Centre. Although there is a modern twist in the seasonings, the main ingredients are very traditional and this is a soup which would have pleased our great-grandparents.

8 ounces beef kidney
A little oil
3–4 slices bacon
1 large onion
2 cloves garlic
1 tablespoon flour
5 cups water
Good dash of Worcestershire sauce
Good dash of soy sauce
1 tablespoon chopped fresh thyme, or 1 teaspoon
    dried thyme
Sea salt (depending on how salty the bacon is) and
    freshly ground black pepper
4–6 slices French bread
¼ cup grated Blarney cheese, Cheddar or other melting cheese

Chop the kidney and wash in plenty of cold, salted water. Drain and dry well on paper. Heat the oil in a good-sized saucepan. Chop the bacon, add to the pan, and sauté for a few minutes. Add the kidney and continue cooking until nicely browned. Peel and finely chop the onion and garlic, stir in and cook until the onion is just soft. Add the flour and cook well until it looks dry and sandy. Gradually add the water, stirring continuously, then add the Worcestershire sauce, soy sauce, thyme and seasoning. Reduce the heat and simmer gently for 30–35 minutes.

Broil the bread slowly until hard and lightly browned. Leave the broiler on. Pour the soup into heatproof bowls, float the bread on top and sprinkle with cheese. Broil until the cheese is bubbling and brown.

Serves 4–6.

→*Lamb and Vegetable Broth* ←

This modern adaptation of traditional mutton broth is one of many excellent recipes from Georgina O'Sullivan of The Meat Centre, an agricultural advisory board in Dublin.

1½ pounds neck of lamb on the bone
1 large onion
2 bay leaves
5 cups water
2–3 carrots
½ turnip
¼ small white cabbage
2–3 leeks
1 tablespoon tomato purée
Freshly chopped parsley
Sea salt and freshly ground black pepper

Trim any excess fat from the meat. Peel and finely chop the onion and put it with the lamb and bay leaves in a large saucepan. Add the water and bring slowly to the boil. Skim and then simmer very gently, covered, for about 1½–2 hours. Meanwhile, peel and dice the carrots and turnip, shred the cabbage, and wash the leeks thoroughly and slice finely.

Lift the lamb onto a board, remove the meat from the bones and cut it into small pieces. Discard the bones and return the meat to the broth. Add the vegetables, tomato purée and parsley; season well. Simmer for another 30 minutes or until the vegetables are tender. Serve with whole-wheat bread.

Serves 6.

⟶ *Pea and Ham Soup* ⟵

Although widely made, this soup has special relevance in Ireland, where the pig once held such an important position that he was referred to as "the gentleman who paid the rent"! I make this soup regularly in winter, whenever there's stock and a few meaty scraps left over after boiling ham or bacon (see pages 34–35).

1 pound dried peas or split green or yellow peas
2 large onions
2 tablespoons bacon fat or butter
1 ham bone and any lean trimmings
Small bunch of fresh herbs — parsley, thyme, bay leaves
2 quarts ham stock
Sea salt and freshly ground black pepper
Crumbled, crisply grilled bacon and/or chopped parsley
   to garnish

Soak the peas overnight, or for at least 3 hours; drain. Peel and finely chop the onions. Melt the bacon fat or butter in a large heavy-bottomed pan and soften the onions in it over gentle heat, without browning. Add the ham bone, drained peas, herbs and stock. Bring to the boil slowly. Then cover and simmer for 2 hours or until the peas are mushy and the soup is a thick purée. Remove the bunch of herbs and the ham bone. Stir the soup well. If it is too thick, thin to the correct consistency with extra stock, water or cream. Dice any ham trimmings and add them to the soup, adjust the seasoning and reheat to a simmer, but don't boil if you have added cream. Serve with a scattering of crumbled bacon and/or chopped parsley.

Serves 6–8.

◆ *Potato Soup* ◆

This most Irish of all soups is not only very good as it is but also incredibly versatile: Use leeks instead of onions and you have leek and potato soup to eat hot, or cold like vichyssoise (not a popular choice in Ireland, I may add!); or liquidize it with strongly flavored herbs such as watercress, sorrel or lovage, which need the body and bland flavor of the potato soup as a base. You can also use it, like Brotchán Foltchep (see page 10) as a base for nettle soup.

> 2 large onions
> 4 tablespoons (½ stick) butter
> 1½ pounds potatoes
> Sea salt and freshly ground black pepper
> 6 cups Chicken Stock (see page 107)
> Freshly chopped chives to garnish
> Cream or milk (optional)

Peel and finely chop the onions. Melt the butter in a large heavy-bottomed pan and turn the onions in it until they are well coated. Cover and let sweat over very low heat. Peel and dice the potatoes. Add to the pan, mix well with the butter and onions, season with salt and freshly ground black pepper and cook, covered, over gentle heat for about 10 minutes until transparent. Add the stock, bring to the boil and simmer for 20–30 minutes or until the vegetables are tender. Remove from the heat and allow to cool slightly, then purée in batches in a blender or food processor. Reheat gently and adjust the seasoning; if the soup seems too thick, add a little extra stock, cream or milk to obtain the right consistency. Serve very hot, scattered with chopped chives.

Serves 6–8.

2. Appetizers and Light Meals

Although the custom of serving a single dish as a separate course at the beginning of a meal is comparatively modern, a surprising number of Irish dishes and specialties are particularly well suited to the role of appetizer, and many are versatile enough to make excellent light meals as well.

⸺→◆ *Angels on Horseback* ◆⸺

Seafood and bacon are often combined in Irish recipes and this is an ideal bite-sized nibble to have with aperitifs — and, of course, perfect fare for a champagne breakfast!

> 24 oysters in their shells
> 24 small slices of smoked bacon
> Fresh lemon juice
> Freshly ground black pepper

Use a blunt-ended oyster knife to shuck the oysters: Insert the end of the knife between the shells near the hinge and work it until you cut through the muscle that holds the shells together. Catch the oyster liquid in a bowl and discard the shells. Put the oysters into a pan with the strained liquid, bring to the boil over gentle heat, simmer very gently for 2 minutes, then drain. Trim the slices of bacon and stretch them by pressing with the back of a knife blade. Sprinkle the oysters with a little lemon juice and freshly ground black pepper, then roll each one up in a bacon slice and thread onto fine skewers. Cook under a hot broiler until the bacon is crisp and sizzling, turning halfway through so both sides are cooked. Push off the skewers and serve hot on cocktail sticks.

Serves 4–6.

➤ *Garlic-Stuffed Mussels* ◆

Mussels are a specialty of Wexford, on the southeast corner of Ireland, but they are also very plentiful all around the coast. Perhaps this recipe sounds more Gallic than Gaelic, but wild herbs, including garlic, have been used in Ireland since time immemorial. This is one of the most popular ways of cooking mussels.

> 4½ pounds fresh mussels in their shells
> 12 tablespoons (1½ sticks) butter
> 4–6 cloves garlic, crushed
> 1 cup fresh white bread crumbs
> Freshly chopped parsley
> Juice of 1 lemon

Wash the mussels in plenty of cold water. Remove beards and discard any with broken shells or ones that don't close when tapped. Put the mussels into a shallow, heavy-bottomed saucepan, without adding any liquid. Cover tightly and cook over high heat for a few minutes, shaking occasionally, until all the mussels have opened. Remove the top shell from each mussel and arrange the bottom shells and the mussels in a shallow flameproof dish. Melt the butter in a pan, add the crushed garlic, bread crumbs, parsley and lemon juice and scatter this mixture over the mussels. Put under a hot broiler or bake in a very hot oven (425°F) for 5–10 minutes until golden brown.

Serves 4–6.

✦ *Kedgeree* ✦

Of Indian origin, kedgeree came to Ireland via England and the landed gentry and quickly established itself as a popular dish for breakfast or high tea.

> 1 pound poached smoked haddock
> 2 cups water
> 1 cup long grain rice
> Sea salt and freshly ground black pepper
> Pinch each of grated nutmeg and cayenne pepper
> 1 onion
> 4 tablespoons (½ stick) butter
> 2 hard-boiled eggs
> Freshly chopped parsley to garnish
> Lemon wedges

Skin the haddock, remove any bones, and flake the flesh with a fork. Set aside. Bring the water to the boil in a large pan. Add the rice and season with salt, freshly ground black pepper, nutmeg and cayenne pepper. Cover closely and cook over low heat for about 25 minutes or until all the water has been absorbed. Meanwhile, peel and finely chop the onion and fry it gently in a little of the butter until soft and transparent. Set aside.

Roughly chop 1 hard-boiled egg and slice the other into neat wedges. Add the remaining butter to the rice and stir in along with the flaked haddock, the onion and the chopped egg. Season to taste and heat the mixture through gently (this can be done on a serving dish in a low oven, if more convenient). To serve, pile the kedgeree up on a warmed dish, sprinkle generously with freshly chopped parsley and arrange the wedges of egg on top. Place the lemon wedges around the base and serve hot with fingers of buttered whole-wheat toast.

Serves 4.

VARIATION
If you have any leftover cooked salmon, substitute it for the haddock.

◆ *Potted Beef* ◆

This simple recipe has been popular with young and old for many generations and has now taken its place as an appetizer, served in a ramekin with hot toast. This version of the traditional recipe was given to me by Valerie McAuliffe of the lovely Neptune Restaurant at Ballyhack — she in turn had it handed down to her from her great-grandmother. Valerie says it can be made with shin or round steak. I infinitely prefer shin, which has much more flavor and suits the cooking method perfectly: When you cook shin gently, without prebrowning, the sinews gradually melt away, adding to the flavor and leaving the meat very tender.

> 1 pound lean boneless beef shank
> Sea salt and freshly ground black pepper
> Clarified butter, as required (see page 110)

Cut the beef into cubes, put it into a casserole with a tight-fitting lid and cover with cold water. Cook in a slow oven (300°F) for 4–5 hours until very tender. Drain the meat, reserving the stock, and mince finely. Add salt and pepper to taste and enough of the stock to make a smooth paste. Divide between 6 ramekins and cover with clarified butter to seal. Chill until required.

Serves 6.

──────◆ *Snaffles Mousse* ◆──────

Snaffles was a famous Dublin restaurant in a Georgian basement, dark, mysterious and famous for its cheese mousse. The restaurant closed in the early 1970s, but it is immortalized in Snaffles mousse, an elegant, deceptively simple dish that is equally good before or after dinner.

> 15-ounce can jellied consommé
> 1 large clove garlic
> 12 ounces cream cheese
> 1 level teaspoon mild curry powder
> Chopped parsley or sliced tomatoes to garnish (optional)

Chill the can of consommé in the refrigerator for at least an hour before opening. Crush the garlic and add to the cream cheese with the curry powder and ¾ cup of the consommé. Process in a blender, divide between 6 ramekins and chill for at least an hour to set. Melt the remaining consommé very slightly so that it is barely warm and just liquefied. Garnish the top of the mousses with parsley or tomato if you like, coat with a thin layer of consommé and leave to set. The mousses can be made up to 3 days ahead and stored, covered, in the refrigerator.

Serves 6.

3. Fish and Seafood

Along the coast fish has always been a regular part of the Irish diet, of course, but great quantities of preserved fish were also sold inland — mostly salt or smoked herrings, but also dried cod and the like. The custom of abstaining from animal products during Lent and on Fridays also meant an increase in the consumption of fish.

Incidentally, it is worth relating here the curious case of the barnacle goose (and possibly the brent goose) being eaten as fish. It was once believed that these geese came not from eggs but from shellfish, and Giraldus Cambrensis, a visitor to Ireland as far back as the twelfth century, said that, "Accordingly in some parts of Ireland bishops and religious men eat them without sin during a fasting time, regarding them as not being flesh, since they were not born of flesh."

The tradition of eating these geese during Lent is well known in many parts of the west of Ireland.

⟶♦ *Black Sole on the Bone* ♦⟵

In Ireland the fish known elsewhere as Dover sole is generally called black sole. It is no relation to lemon sole, a much softer and less expensive fish. Black sole is a treat by any standards. It is superb grilled or pan-fried on the bone and served plain, with salad or vegetables as a separate course or at least on a separate plate. Unusual, for a flat fish, black sole is best eaten two or three days old, when the flavor has intensified. Get the coarse black skin removed for you, but retain the white one as it adds flavor and keeps the cooked fish in shape. Cook the skin side first, if grilling, the reverse if pan-frying, as it will be easier to serve.

> 4 medium-sized Dover sole, cleaned and gutted
> A little butter and oil (if frying), or melted butter (if grilling)
> Juice of ½ lemon
> Freshly ground black pepper
> Finely chopped fresh parsley
> Lemon wedges

Wash the fish and dry thoroughly with paper towels. Heat the grill or a heavy frying pan; oil the grille rack if using, or heat an equal quantity of butter and oil in the pan. Season the fish on both sides with lemon juice and freshly ground black pepper, brush with melted butter if grilling, then cook for 4 or 5 minutes, depending on thickness; turn carefully and cook the second side until the flesh is opaque and comes away easily from the bone when tested with the tip of a knife. Carefully transfer the fish to warmed plates, pour over any pan juices, if frying, scatter with parsley and garnish with lemon wedges. New potatoes, served separately, are delicious with the sole, in addition to a mixed green leaf salad.

Serves 4.

VARIATION
You can cook good, firm medium-sized flounder or lemon sole in the same way.

———◆ *Dublin Lawyer* ◆———

This traditional dish used to be made with raw lobster but it is perhaps a better idea to boil it first.

>1 2-pound live lobster
>12 tablespoons (1½ sticks) butter
>3 ounces Irish whiskey
>⅓ cup heavy cream
>Sea salt and freshly ground black pepper

Cook the lobster lightly and tear off the claws. Split the body in half lengthwise, just slightly to the right of the center line to avoid cutting into the digestive tract. Remove the gray matter from the head of the shell and discard. Remove the digestive tract right down the length of the body and discard. Lift the flesh from the tail — it usually comes out in one piece. You don't need to wash the shells, but keep them warm. Tear the two joints in the claw to separate them and, using a lobster pick or a small knife, scoop out the flesh. With the back of a heavy knife, hit the claw near the pincers, rotating the claw and hitting about four times until the claw can be pulled open. Remove the flesh and cut into bite-sized pieces.

Melt the butter in a saucepan over a low heat. Add the lobster and turn it gently in the butter to warm through. Warm the whiskey, pour it over the lobster and set alight. Once the flames have died down add the cream and heat gently without allowing the sauce to boil, then taste and season with a little salt (if necessary) and a grinding of black pepper. Turn the hot mixture into the warm shells and serve immediately.

Serves 2.

———— ◆ *Fish Cakes* ◆ ————

A well-made fish cake is a joy and I'm delighted to see them creeping back onto restaurant menus again after years of "school dinners" image. Make fish cakes with any white fish, fresh or smoked, or a mixture. This is another dish that makes a little fish go a long way.

> 1 pound fresh or smoked cod, haddock or pollock
> Wedge of lemon, small bay leaf, parsley sprigs
> 2 tablespoons butter
> 1 onion, finely chopped
> 2 cups mashed potatoes, seasoned with salt and pepper and
>   with enough milk to produce a creamy consistency
> 2 tablespoons freshly chopped parsley
> Freshly ground black pepper
> Quick oatmeal for coating
> Butter and oil for frying

Rinse the fish, cut into manageable pieces and put into a pan with just enough cold water to cover. Add the lemon, bay leaf and parsley, and bring slowly to a boil. Reduce heat and simmer gently for 5–7 minutes until the fish is tender, then remove it and drain well. When cool enough to handle, flake the flesh and discard the skin and bones.

Melt the butter in a large saucepan, add the chopped onion and cook gently for a few minutes without browning. When the onion has softened, add the flaked fish, mashed potato and chopped parsley, and season to taste with freshly ground black pepper. Turn the mixture out onto a worktop generously covered with quick oatmeal and divide into 8 portions. Form into flat cakes and coat them well with the oatmeal. Heat a little butter and an equal quantity of oil in a heavy frying pan or griddle, add the fish cakes (in batches if necessary) and fry until golden brown on both sides. Drain and serve immediately — Parsley Sauce is the traditional accompaniment (see page 109).

Serves 4.

Herring Fillets in Oatmeal with Apple

This simple dish is traditional in Scotland as well as Ireland and is one of the most delicious ways of cooking herring. Make sure all the fine bones have been removed from the fillets before coating them.

> 8 herring fillets
> Seasoned flour
> 1 egg, beaten
> 1⅓ cups fine quick oatmeal
> Oil for frying
> 2 eating apples
> 2 tablespoons butter

Wash the fillets and pat dry with paper towels. Check that all bones have been removed. Toss the fillets in seasoned flour, then dip them in the beaten egg and coat with the oats. Heat a little oil in a heavy-bottomed frying pan and fry the fillets, a few at a time, until golden brown. Drain on kitchen paper and keep warm. Core the apples, but do not peel; slice quite thinly. Fry gently in the butter in a separate pan until just softened, then serve the herring fillets garnished with the apple slices.

Serves 4.

VARIATIONS
Cook mackerel fillets in the same way.
Serve applesauce instead of the sliced apples.

Jugged Kippers

Kippers are most popular for breakfast, served with scrambled eggs, but they are also good at an old-fashioned high tea or Irish supper — a meal that has virtually died out in urban areas but is still going strong in the country. Jugging is much the same as poaching, except that the only equipment needed is a jug and a kettle.

> 4 kippers, whole or filleted
> Freshly ground black pepper
> 2 tablespoons butter

Select a jug tall enough for the kippers to be completely immersed when the water is added — an old-fashioned one with a hinged lid is ideal. If the heads are still on, remove them. Put the fish into the jug, tails up, then cover them with boiling water. Leave for about 5 minutes or until tender. Drain well and serve on warmed plates with a grinding of black pepper and a knob of butter on each kipper, accompanied by freshly made whole-wheat soda bread, or toast, and scrambled eggs if you like.

Serves 4.

———→ *Poached Salmon* ←———

Use a fish poacher if at all possible: It's the perfect shape to accommodate the salmon using the minimum of liquid and has a removable rack for lifting the fish in and out of the cooking liquor without damaging it. Some kitchen shops rent this kind of special equipment, otherwise it is worth considering buying a fish poacher between a group of friends.

> 1 whole salmon, cleaned and gutted
> Court bouillon (see page 108) or
>   salted water
> Fresh parsley and lemon wedges to garnish
> Special equipment: poacher big enough to
>   hold the whole fish without bending

Wash the fish well but do not scale it and, of course, leave the head and tail intact. The cooking time depends on the thickness of the fish, so measure it at its thickest point and allow 10 minutes per

1 inch of thickness. Lay the salmon in the fish poacher and add just enough cold court bouillon or salted water (1 tablespoon salt per quart) to cover. Put over a moderate heat and gradually bring up to a gentle simmer. Do not allow it to boil as the high temperature will harm the delicate flavor and texture of the fish. Simmer for the time calculated — this should work out at about 15–20 minutes for a medium-sized fish (6½–9 pounds), 25–30 minutes for a large one (10–14 pounds). Test by lifting the flesh off the backbone at the thickest point, where the flesh meets the head; when cooked, the flesh will come away from the bone easily with no sign of blood.

Lift the salmon out, drain for a minute or two, then slide it off its rack onto a warmed serving dish. Garnish with lots of fresh parsley and lemon wedges and take it straight to the table. The skin helps keep the fish warm and moist, so only peel it back as far as necessary as you serve; remove all the flesh from the top half first, then remove the backbone as neatly as you can and continue with the bottom layer. Serve with new potatoes and hollandaise sauce.

A 6½–7 pound fish will serve 10–12.

VARIATION

Cold Poached Salmon: Remove the fish poacher from the heat when it comes to the boil and cover with a tight-fitting lid. The salmon will cook gently in the liquor as it cools, producing a very tender, juicy, cold fish. When just cool, remove from the cooking liquor and drain on the poaching rack. Line a suitable serving dish with lettuce, watercress, cucumber and lemon wedges. Slide the salmon carefully onto the dish. Peel off the skin, but leave the head and tail intact. Garnish as you like and serve with mayonnaise.

✦ *Sea Pie* ✦

Sea pie sounds much more intriguing than fish pie and, when well made, it is absolutely delicious. Children especially love it because of its crispy top and the reassuring absence of bones. You can make it with any white fish, such as cod or haddock, but it is particularly good made with a mixture of fresh and smoked fish — ideal winter fare when the fishing fleets are hampered by gales and fresh fish is in short supply. As sea pie is another name for the oyster-catcher, a few oysters could even be included!

> 1 pound haddock or cod fillets
> ½ pound smoked haddock or cod
> ½ cup milk
> ½ cup water
> A slice of lemon, small bay leaf and parsley stalks

Sauce:

> 2 tablespoons butter
> ¼ cup flour
> 2 heaped tablespoons freshly chopped parsley
> Lemon juice to taste
> Freshly ground black pepper

Topping:

> 2 cups mashed potatoes, seasoned with salt and pepper and
>   with enough milk to produce a creamy consistency
> 2 tablespoons butter

Rinse the fish, cut it into manageable pieces and put into a pan with the milk, water, lemon, bay leaf and parsley stalks. Bring slowly to a boil. Then simmer gently for about 15 minutes until tender. Strain and reserve 1 cup of the cooking liquid for the sauce. Leave the fish until cool enough to handle. Then flake the flesh and discard the skin and bones. Set aside.

To make the sauce, melt the butter in a heavy-bottomed pan, add the flour and cook for 1–2 minutes over low heat, then gradually add the reserved cooking liquid, stirring well to make a smooth sauce. Simmer gently for 1–2 minutes, then draw off the heat and stir in the flaked fish, chopped parsley and lemon juice. Season to taste with freshly ground black pepper. Turn into a buttered 3-pint pie dish or shallow casserole, cover with the mashed potato and dot with the butter. Cook in a preheated moderately hot oven (375°F) for about 20 minutes or until thoroughly heated through. The top should be golden brown and crunchy. Brown under the grille for a few moments or leave in the oven a little longer, if necessary.

Serves 4–5.

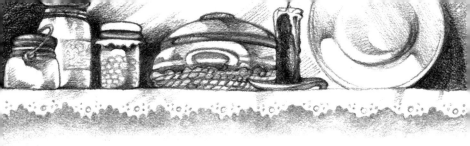

4. Meat and Poultry

PORK

The pig was probably the first domestic animal to be brought to Ireland and, although its absolute supremacy as a source of meat was later to be challenged by cattle and sheep, its popularity has never waned. Until quite recently pork butchers specializing in every possible edible product of the pig were to be found in every town and village but, although they haven't died out completely, the general butcher and, of course, the supermarket have tended to supersede them. However, every part of the animal is still put to good use and many country people can remember the time when most rural households killed at least one pig a year. It was a complicated business, with the men and women each having their

particular jobs. The men did the killing, cleaning, butchery and salting, while the women dealt with the trotters, internal organs and any other parts that were to be cooked fresh. The hams were usually put into a blend of salt, saltpetre and brown sugar for several days and then smoked, preferably over oak chippings. Afterwards, they were hung up on iron hooks from a beam called "the meat stick" that ran across the kitchen, where turf smoke from the open hearth gave it a special Irish flavor. Black pudding was made from the blood, chopped fat, oatmeal, herbs and seasoning; this mixture was loosely filled into lengths of the cleaned intestines, tied in circles and then boiled. Next came "the parcelling out," when portions of the fresh meat and black pudding were sorted out for the neighbors and delivered by the children of the house — this was a very important custom, as a number of households exchanging gifts after a killing meant that fresh meat was available much more often.

Although not specifically associated with any particular festival, pork and ham have always been regular features at every Irish festive occasion. When Lent was strictly observed, bacon was often the main item of the festive supper on Shrove Tuesday and, along with beef, it played an important part in the Harvest Home celebrations at the end of September. In addition to the fact that the pig is the smallest of the domestic farm animals and therefore convenient for family use, perhaps its incredible versatility explains the enduring popularity of pork — the various cuts all get different treatments, providing great variety of flavor and texture and, unlike other animals, the meat is so tender that any fresh cut is suitable for virtually all cooking methods, including roasting and grilling.

➤ *Dublin Coddle* ✦

This traditional dish is every bit as comforting as it sounds. For hundreds of years it has been the Saturday-night drinkers' friend — absolutely forgiving and always welcoming whatever the time! I first made it as a student in Belfast, using this recipe from Theodora FitzGibbon's lovely book, *A Taste of Ireland*. It is utterly Irish and, as Theodora points out in her introduction, combines two foods known since the earliest Irish literature: "Bacon (tinne or sensaille) is mentioned many times in the medieval Vision of MacConglinne, as are sausages, particularly one called Maroc, and another called Indrechtán. Leeks and oatmeal were no doubt used in the earliest form of Coddle but, since the eighteenth century, potatoes and onions have supplanted them."

> 8 ¼-inch-thick slices ham or bacon
> 8 pork sausages
> 1 quart boiling water
> 4 large onions
> 2 pounds potatoes
> 4 rounded tablespoons freshly chopped parsley
> Sea salt and freshly ground black pepper

Cut the ham or bacon slices into large chunks and cook with the sausages in the boiling water for 5 minutes. Drain but reserve the liquid. Peel and thinly slice the onions and potatoes. Put the meat into a large saucepan or ovenproof dish with the onions, potatoes and parsley. Season to taste and add enough of the stock to barely cover. Lay a piece of parchment paper on top and then put on the lid and simmer gently, or cook in a very slow oven (250°F) for about an hour or until the liquid is reduced by half and all the ingredients are cooked but not mushy (this will take longer in the oven than on top of the stove). Serve hot with fresh soda bread and glasses of stout.

Serves 4 very generously or 8 normal portions.

◆ *Limerick Ham* ◆

Ham smoked over oak chips and juniper berries was a famous speciality of Limerick in the eighteenth century, and ham — the name refers only to the leg, all the rest is called bacon — is still one of Ireland's most highly regarded foods. It can be boiled and served cold, but it is most popular baked and served hot with parsley sauce. Some of the milk for the sauce can be replaced with hot ham stock, which makes the sauce easier to blend, lighter and more flavorsome. I often add a few crushed juniper berries to the cooking pot along with the peppercorns. Cooking ham or gammon (the joint taken from a side of bacon as opposed to pork) in the following way gives it its characteristic sweetish flavor and juicy, tender texture.

> About 4½ pounds smoked ham
> 1 rounded tablespoon brown sugar or honey
> 6–8 black peppercorns, lightly crushed
> 6–8 juniper berries, lightly crushed
> 2 rounded tablespoons fresh bread crumbs
> ½ level teaspoon ground cloves
> 1 rounded tablespoon dark brown sugar
> 1 tablespoon honey
> Parsley Sauce to serve (see page 109)

Place the ham in a large pan. Cover generously with cold water and let soak overnight or for at least 8 hours. Drain, replace with fresh water to cover and add the spoonful of sugar or honey and the lightly crushed peppercorns and juniper berries. Bring slowly to the boil, skim and reduce the heat to a simmer. Cook gently for 20 minutes per pound, keeping the water at a simmer. If the ham is to be eaten cold it will be juicier if left to cool in the cooking liquid.

Preheat a moderate oven (350°F). Remove the ham from the pan, drain, reserving the stock, and remove the skin. If the layer of fat underneath is very thick, trim it, but leave enough to keep the ham moist and provide a tasty crust. Mix the fresh bread crumbs, ground cloves and brown sugar together well, then bind with the honey — melt it slightly if it is too hard to mix. Spread this mixture evenly over the fat, pressing well in. Put the ham into a roasting tin with about 1 cup of the ham stock and bake for 30–40 minutes until the crust is brown and crunchy. Let rest for a few minutes before carving. Serve with Parsley Sauce.

Serves 6–8.

VARIATION

To serve cold, let the ham cool in its cooking liquid, then drain well and remove the skin, as above. Cover the fat evenly with equal quantities of fine oven-dried bread crumbs and brown sugar.

NOTE: Use the reserved ham liquid as stock for making Pea and Ham Soup (see page 14).

—▸ *Michael Clifford's Cruibíns* ◂—

Cruibíns, or crubeens as they are also spelled, must be one of the most traditional of all Irish specialties. However you spell it, it means pig's trotters, and it is by no means a thing of the past. As Dublin Coddle waited patiently at home to be consumed late on a Saturday night, so cruibíns offered sustenance meanwhile in the pubs — and still do in some country districts.

> 4 cured cruibíns (pigs' feet)
> Cheesecloth
> 1 cup white wine
> Water
> 1 bay leaf or bouquet garni
> 6 crushed peppercorns
> 1 teaspoon white wine vinegar
> 1 carrot, chopped
> 1 onion, chopped
> 1 stalk celery, chopped
> 3–4 juniper berries

Tie the cruibíns in pairs, with a soft wooden stick between them and using cheesecloth to bind them together. This will keep their shape and look more attractive. Put the cruibíns into a large saucepan with all the other ingredients and cover with water. Bring to a boil and simmer very gently, covered, for at least 4–5 hours, adding water as necessary, until tender. Untie the cruibíns and serve cold with an herb vinaigrette, or serve hot, coated with bread crumbs, seasoned with nutmeg, allspice or cinnamon, browned in a hot oven or under the broiler.

Serves 4.

◆ *Pork Ciste* ◆

This is a very traditional dish but visitors are not likely to come across it unless, perhaps, in one of the specialist Irish restaurants that are now beginning to make an impact. "Ciste" means cake and refers to the suet crust topping, which serves several purposes: During cooking the crust keeps the steam in and ensures that the meat is kept moist and tender, then, at the table, it provides a contrast of flavor and texture, and is filling. In short, it's a well-balanced one-pot meal and definitely due for revival. Cook it on top of the stove or in the oven. If the latter, remove the lid for the last half hour of cooking to brown and crisp the ciste. Lamb or mutton can also be used for a ciste, with flavorings adapted to suit. In this one apples and cider are the perfect partners.

> 6 lean pork chops
> 2 pork kidneys (or use beef kidneys)
> 4 tablespoons (½ stick) butter
> 1 tablespoon oil
> 1 large onion
> 2–3 carrots
> 1 cooking apple
> 1 rounded tablespoon freshly chopped parsley
> 1 teaspoon freshly chopped thyme
> Sea salt and freshly ground black pepper
> About 2 cups hard cider

For the ciste (suet crust):

> 2 cups self-rising flour
> Good pinch of salt
> 4 ounces shredded suet
> ½–⅔ cup golden raisins
> About ½ cup milk to mix

Trim any fat off the pork chops; skin and halve the kidneys, remove the cores and chop them. Heat the butter and oil in a large, heavy-bottomed flameproof casserole and brown the meat in it. Meanwhile, peel and slice the onion, carrots and cooking apple. Remove the meat from the casserole and set aside. Lightly cook the vegetables in the same fat for a minute or two, then pile them up in the middle of the casserole with the kidneys, cooking apple and chopped herbs, and push the chops in around the edges. Season with salt and pepper and add just enough cider to cover the vegetables. Cover with a tight-fitting lid, bring to the boil and simmer for half an hour.

Meanwhile, make the suet pastry: Put the flour, salt, suet and raisins in a bowl and, mixing with a fork, add enough milk to make a fairly stiff dough. On a floured worktop, roll the dough out to fit the top of the casserole, then press it down on top of the meat and vegetables, leaving room on top to allow for rising. Cover with buttered parchment paper and the lid and continue to simmer for another 1½ hours. Alternatively, cook in a moderate oven (350°F) for the same time, removing the lid and parchment paper for the last half hour to allow the ciste to brown. To serve, loosen around the edge of the ciste with a knife and cut it into 6 portions. Put one chop and some of the kidney and vegetable mixture on each plate with a wedge of crust.

Serves 6.

⟶ ✦ *Stuffed Pork Steaks* ✦ ⟶

Pork steak is a cut of meat peculiar to Ireland and known as pork fillet or tenderloin in Britain. It is lean, tender and very versatile, but expensive — so stuffing it is the traditional way to make the meat go further. Although they are sometimes larger, an average tenderloin weighs about 12 ounces to 1 pound and, if grilled, serves two — whereas two stuffed steaks will serve six.

> 2 evenly sized pork tenderloins, about 14 ounces each
> Softened butter, as required

Stuffing:
> 2 cups fresh white bread crumbs
> 2 rounded tablespoons freshly chopped parsley
> 1 rounded teaspoon freshly chopped thyme
> 1 medium onion
> 2 tablespoons butter
> 1 small egg
> Finely grated zest and juice of 1 small lemon or orange
> Sea salt and freshly ground black pepper

Before stuffing, prepare the steaks to make them into fairly thin, rectangular pieces. Slit them along their length with a sharp knife, being careful not to cut right through, then hold out each of the flaps this has produced and slit them lengthwise in the same way, without cutting right through. Flatten out gently.

Next, make the stuffing. Mix the bread crumbs, parsley and thyme in a bowl. Peel and finely chop the onion, melt the butter and lightly beat the egg; then add to the bowl. Grate the citrus zest into the bowl, add a sprinkling of salt and pepper and mix all the ingredients together with a fork, including as much of the squeezed juice as is required to bind the stuffing without making it sloppy. Set aside any leftover juice for flavoring the gravy later. The pork steaks can now be stuffed, either individually or together. To cook them individually, divide the stuffing mixture in half and lay it down the center of each steak; fold the flaps up toward the middle and secure with string or skewers to make a roll. Alternatively, turn all the stuffing onto one of the steaks, spread evenly, then cover with the second steak; secure with twine or skewers. In both cases, use cotton string, as synthetic ones will melt in the oven. Whichever method is chosen, rub the steaks with a little softened butter, season lightly with salt and pepper and put into a shallow dish or roasting pan with about 1 cup water to prevent the meat from drying out too much during cooking. Cover with a lid or foil and cook in a moderate oven (350°F) for about an hour, turning and basting halfway through the cooking time, if possible. Remove the steaks and keep warm while you make a gravy by reducing or thickening the juices in the roasting pan, adding any leftover citrus juice.

Serves 6.

LAMB AND MUTTON

◆ Irish Stew ◆

Now known as Ireland's national dish, there must be as many versions of Irish stew as there are cooks still making it. Aside from the meat (which may or may not be cooked on the bone) there are longstanding arguments about the correct ingredients for an authentic Irish stew and, especially, whether or not carrots are permitted. This is Theodora FitzGibbon's version, from *A Taste of Ireland*, and in her introduction she says: "It was originally made with either mutton or kid (no farmer would be so foolhardy as to use his lambs for it), potatoes and onions. The pure flavor is spoiled if carrots, turnips or pearl barley are added, or if it is too liquid. A good Irish stew should be thick and creamy, not swimming in juice like soup."

> 3 pounds thick shoulder lamb chops
> 2 pounds potatoes
> 1 pound onions
> 1 rounded tablespoon freshly chopped
>   parsley and thyme, mixed
> Sea salt and freshly ground black pepper
> ½ cup water

Trim the meat of fat, bone and gristle and cut it into fairly large pieces. Peel and slice the potatoes and onions. Put a layer of potatoes in a casserole, then the herbs, the sliced meat and finally the onion, seasoning each layer well with salt and pepper. Repeat the layers, finishing with a layer of potatoes. Pour the liquid over, cover with a sheet of foil, then the lid, and either bake in a very slow oven (250°F) or simmer very gently on top of the stove for about 2 hours, shaking the pot from time to time so that the ingredients don't stick. Add a little more liquid if it seems to be getting very dry.

Another method is to put the trimmed chops around the edge of a saucepan and put the sliced onions and small potatoes with herbs and seasonings into the middle. Add the water and cook as above.

Serves 4.

Boiled Mutton
with Caper Sauce

This used to be a very popular dish, but it has disappeared in the second half of this century only because of the fashion for eating tender young animals, which are better suited to fast cooking methods. In the current mood of renewed respect for regional food and traditional dishes, mutton is certain to be reassessed, and many people who have always thought of it as inferior to lamb may be surprised how good it is.

> 4 pounds leg or shoulder of mutton
> 1 teaspoon salt
> Carrots, turnips and onions

Sauce:

> 4 tablespoons (½ stick) butter
> ½ cup flour
> 1 cup milk
> 1 tablespoon capers
> 1 teaspoon caper vinegar (from the caper jar)
> Sea salt and freshly ground black pepper

Wipe and trim the meat, making sure there is no excess fat on it. In a large, heavy saucepan bring to the boil enough water to cover the roast. Add the salt and the meat to the pan. Boil for 5 minutes to seal in the juices, then skim and reduce the heat to a gentle simmer for 20 minutes per pound. Cut the vegetables into neat chunks and add to the meat. If they are old, they may need an hour or more to cook; if young, add them only half an hour or so before the mutton is done. When the mutton is ready, lift it onto a hot serving dish, arrange the vegetables around it and keep it warm while you make the sauce. Reserve 1 cup of the mutton stock.

Prepare the sauce in the same way as White Sauce (see page 108), using the reserved mutton stock but adding the capers and caper vinegar to the cooked sauce. Season to taste with salt and pepper. Serve the mutton thickly sliced; surround with the vegetables and pour the caper sauce over.

◆ *Dingle Pies* ◆

These small pies are not unlike Cornish pasties. They are traditional in Dingle for special occasions such as Lammas Day, August 1, which marks the first day of the harvest, and also for the famous three-day cattle market, Puck Fair, at Killorglin, which is very much alive and well. The "king" of the fair is a billy goat bedecked with ribbons and chained by the horns on a high platform. There "garlanded by greenery" (supplied with a generous stock of cabbages), he presides over the fair as a symbol of fertility and good luck.

There are numerous recipes for mutton pies in the Dingle area; the pastry was shortened with dripping or mutton fat and the pies were sometimes boiled in mutton stock. Nowadays, shortcrust pastry is usually made with butter or a mixture of butter and lard and the pies are baked in the oven, as in this modern variation that contains more vegetables than the traditional recipe.

> Double quantity of Shortcrust Pastry (see page 110)
> 1 pound boneless mutton or lamb
> 1 large onion
> 2 carrots
> 1 potato
> 2 stalks celery
> Sea salt and freshly ground black pepper
> 1 egg, beaten

First make the pastry and leave it in the refrigerator to rest while you prepare the other ingredients. Trim any fat or gristle from the meat and cut into small dice. Peel the onion, carrots and potato and cut into small dice. Trim the celery and cut into similar dice. Mix the meat and vegetables together and season with salt and pepper. Preheat a moderate oven (350°F).

Reserve a third of the pastry to make the pie lids. Roll out the rest and, using a small plate as a guide and re-rolling the pastry as necessary, cut out 6 circles. Divide the meat and vegetable mixture between them, piling it neatly in the middle of each. Roll out the remaining pastry and cut out 6 smaller circles. Lay these on top of the piles of meat. Dampen the edges of the pastry bases, bring the pastry up around the meat, pleat it to fit the lid and pinch the two edges together. Make a little hole in the top of each pie for steam to escape, then brush with the beaten egg and slide the pies onto baking sheets. Bake in the preheated oven for an hour. Eat hot or cold. The original pies made a handy portable meal for farmers and fishermen, so they're ideal for picnics.

Serves 6.

VARIATION

If you happen to have lamb gravy left over from a roast, mix a little in with the raw ingredients — it will make the pies juicier.

BEEF

Irish stew may be regarded as the Irish national dish but beef is the traditional highlight of festive meals. Beef was traditional on Easter Sunday, when better-off farmers "killed a beef" for the festival and sent presents of portions to their poorer neighbors. Very often the cow had been slaughtered in the early winter and salted down — special roasts of this were eaten at the farm on festival days, while portions were sent to the laborers and poorer people who had no meat of their own. This custom goes back beyond living memory but it is the origin of the Irish-American belief, which apparently still survives in America, that corned beef and cabbage is the main Irish festive meal.

At Christmas, turkey has taken pride of place on the dinner table in recent years, but spiced beef has been the traditional seasonal treat for many generations and most Irish households will still have a piece ready prepared for St. Stephen's Day and for any entertaining planned for the Christmas and New Year holiday. It always makes a welcome change from turkey and shows no sign of becoming a thing of the past. Meat of any kind was cause for celebration for poor families at one time, of course, but good beef was a treat all around, as most of the best beef has always been exported from Ireland, and cattle were generally kept mainly for their dairy produce. A cow was destined for the table only when it was too old for milking.

Beefsteak and Kidney Pie with Suet Crust

The classic steak and kidney pie is another way of stretching a modest amount of meat. This dish has stood the test of time and, despite being out of fashion over the last decade or so, is once again becoming popular. If you have never had a homemade steak and kidney pie with a real suet crust, try this and give yourself a treat.

> 1½ pounds beef chuck blade steak
> 8 ounces beef kidney
> 2 onions
> 1 clove garlic
> 1⅔ cups mushrooms
> 1 tablespoon flour
> 2 tablespoons oil
> 1½ cups water
> 1 tablespoon tomato purée (optional)
> 1 tablespoon Worcestershire sauce
> ½ teaspoon dried mixed herbs
> Sea salt and freshly ground black pepper

Suet crust:

> 1 cup self-rising flour
> 2 ounces shredded suet
> Sea salt and freshly ground black pepper
> Water to mix
> A little beaten egg or milk

Remove any bones from the rib steak, trim the meat and chop into fairly small, bite-sized pieces. Remove the skin and core from the kidney, then chop it. Peel and chop the onions, peel and crush the garlic, wipe and halve the mushrooms.

Toss the meat in the flour. Heat the oil in a large pan and brown the meat, a few pieces at a time. As it browns, transfer it to a plate. Add the kidney, onion and garlic to the pan and cook for a few minutes, then add the mushrooms. Mix the water, tomato purée, if using, Worcestershire sauce and herbs together and pour into the pan.

Return the meat to the pan, stir well and season, then cover and simmer for about 1½ hours or until the meat is tender. When the meat is cooked, pour the contents of the pan into a 1-quart dish and allow to cool. Preheat a hot oven (400°F).

Make up the suet crust: Mix the dry ingredients lightly with a fork, then add enough cold water to make a smooth elastic dough. Set aside for 5 minutes, then roll out to make a piece about 1 inch bigger all around than the top of the pie dish. Cut off this excess, dampen the rim of the pie dish and press the pastry strip onto it. Then dampen the strip and lay the pastry lid on top, pressing it down and sealing around the edge. Flute the edges, make a small hole in the center, decorate with any leftovers made into pastry leaves if you have time, brush with a little beaten egg or milk, and bake in the pre-heated oven until the pastry is golden brown.

Serves 4–6.

➞ *Braised Steaks in Guinness* ⬅

Most people find prime steak prohibitively expensive for family meals or even casual entertaining. Slightly cheaper cuts, such as round steak, are delicious braised, however, and dishes like this are no hardship as an alternative.

> A little good oil for frying
> 4 round steaks
> 1 cup button mushrooms
> 1 onion
> 8 ounces Guinness
> Sprig of thyme
> Few strips of orange peel (optional)
> Sea salt and freshly ground black pepper

Heat the oven to moderate (350°F). Heat a little oil in a large frying pan and brown the steaks quickly on both sides. Remove from the pan and set aside. Trim the mushrooms, halve or quarter them if necessary, then peel and finely chop the onion. Add a little more oil to the frying pan if necessary and toss the mushrooms and onion in it for a few minutes until they just begin to color, then spread the mixture over the base of a medium-sized baking dish. Lay the steaks over the mushroom and onion mixture. Barely cover with Guinness, add the thyme and orange peel, if using, and season well. Cover the dish with a lid or foil and braise in the preheated oven for 1–1½ hours or until the meat is tender. Baked potatoes, which can be cooked in the oven at the same time, are ideal for soaking up the delicious juices.

Serves 4.

Corned Beef with
⟶ *Dumplings and Cabbage* ⟵

This was the traditional favorite for Easter and has more recently become associated with St. Patrick's Day. Brisket can be used, but remember to ask your butcher if it needs to be soaked. If in doubt, soak in cold water overnight, then drain and replace with fresh water before cooking. The traditional accompaniments for corned beef are cabbage and Parsley Sauce (see page 109), but dumplings were sometimes included as well to make a more filling meal that would stretch the meat for a big family.

> 3 pounds corned brisket
> 1 onion
> 4 cloves
> 2 bay leaves
> 8 peppercorns

Dumplings:

> 1 small onion
> 1 cup self-rising flour
> 2 tablespoons freshly chopped parsley
> 2 ounces shredded beef suet
> Sea salt and freshly ground black pepper
> A little flour
> Parsley Sauce (see page 109)
> 1 cabbage (any sort), shredded

Soak the meat if necessary. When ready to cook, drain, put in a saucepan and cover with fresh cold water. Peel the onion and stick the cloves into it, then add it to the saucepan with the bay leaves and peppercorns. Bring slowly to the boil, cover and simmer for 2 hours or until the meat is tender.

Meanwhile, make the dumplings: Peel and very finely chop the onion and mix with the flour, parsley, suet and seasoning, then add just enough water to make a soft but not too sticky dough. Dust your hands with a little flour and shape the dough into 12 small dumplings. When the meat is cooked, remove it from the pan and keep warm. Bring the cooking liquid to a brisk boil, put in the dumplings and cook briskly, covered, for 15 minutes, making sure they don't stop boiling. Serve the dumplings with Parsley Sauce (see page 109), the beef and shredded cabbage, which should be lightly cooked in a little of the stock. (The remaining stock can be used for soup.)

Serves 6.

VARIATION

Horseradish or mustard sauce: Apart from the traditional parsley sauce, a light horseradish or mustard sauce goes well with the beef and is quicker to make: Whip ½ cup heavy cream, then stir in 1 tablespoon mild Dijon mustard or horseradish relish and 2 teaspoons lemon juice; season to taste with salt and pepper.

⟶◆ *Pan-Fried Gaelic Steaks* ◆⟵

"A good steak" is undoubtedly the nation's favorite food, and many an Irishman looks forward to a good thick sirloin on a Saturday night as the high point of his week. As with other very simple dishes, top-quality raw materials and a good sense of timing are essential for success. A small, thick steak is easier to cook well than a large, thin one and testing by the feel of the meat is better than relying on timing alone.

> Four 8–12 ounce sirloin steaks, at room temperature
> Freshly ground black pepper
> 1 tablespoon butter
> 1 teaspoon oil
> ¼ cup Irish whiskey
> 1 cup heavy cream
> Sea salt

Heat a heavy frying pan, preferably cast-iron, over a high heat. Dry the steaks with paper towels and season with black pepper. When the pan is really hot add the butter and oil. When the butter is hot and foaming, add the steaks one at a time so that the fat maintains its heat and seals the meat quickly. Lower the heat to moderate and leave undisturbed for half the cooking time: 3–4 minutes for rare, 4–5 minutes for medium, 5–6 minutes for well done, depending on the thickness of the steak — very thick steaks will take longer. Turn only once. To test if your timing is right, press down gently in the middle of the steak — if the meat gives easily, it's rare; if there is some resistance but the meat still feels soft, it's medium; if it feels firm, the steak is well done. When the steaks are cooked to your liking, remove them to warmed plates. Pour off the fat from the pan and discard. Add the whiskey and stir around to scrape off all the sediment from the base of the pan. Reduce slightly, then add the cream and simmer over a low heat for a few minutes until the cream thickens. Season to taste with salt and pepper, pour the sauce around or over the steaks as preferred and serve immediately.

Serves 4.

Shin Beef Stew
with Dumplings

Large Irish families, especially those with large country appetites, have always needed hearty, filling dishes, and clever cooks would use every trick in the book to make small amounts of meat feed as many mouths as possible. As a result, many Irish dishes include (and are often enhanced by) inexpensive and nutritious "fillers" — grains and legumes from earliest times, then rice and, more recently, pasta. Pastry of all kinds served the same purpose and, where a pastry covering wasn't practical, similar ingredients were often made up into tasty dumplings for all kinds of stews. This one, made with shin of beef, is especially good and very simple — providing you don't make the mistake of browning it first as for other cuts, which makes it tough. The sinews melt down during the long gentle cooking and make an exceptionally flavorsome gravy.

1–1½ pounds boneless beef shank
2 large onions
4 large carrots
4 stalks celery
2 cloves garlic (optional)
1½ cups water
2 rounded tablespoons tomato purée
Sea salt and freshly ground black pepper

Dumplings:
¾ cup self-rising flour
½ cup fresh white bread crumbs
2 ounces shredded suet
Pinch of sea salt
1 tablespoon freshly chopped parsley
1 teaspoon freshly chopped thyme
Cold water to mix

1 teaspoon corn starch dissolved in 1 tablespoon water, if required (see method)

Cut the meat into bite-sized chunks and put it into a large, heavy-bottomed saucepan. Peel and slice the onions, scrape the carrots and cut them into large chunks, cut the celery into large pieces, and crush the garlic, if using. Add the vegetables to the pan. Mix the water and tomato purée together. Pour it over the meat and vegetables and add a sprinkling of salt and a good grinding of black pepper. Cover tightly and simmer very gently over a low heat for 2 hours or until the meat is tender. Check the pan occasionally to make sure it hasn't stopped simmering and add a little extra water if it seems to be reducing too much.

Meanwhile, make the dumplings. Mix the dry ingredients thoroughly, then add just enough water to bind them. Divide the mixture into about 12 equal portions and, with floured hands, roll them into balls. When the meat is tender, add the dumplings, bring back up to the boil and cook, uncovered, for about 15 minutes. If the gravy seems too thin, stir in the corn starch and boil for a couple of minutes before serving. Serve with potatoes boiled in their jackets.

Serves 4–6.

◆ *Traditional Spiced Beef* ◆

Although the list of ingredients is long and you need to allow about ten days to make spiced beef in the traditional way, it isn't difficult — and it is much cheaper as well as nicer than the prepared ones you can buy from butchers. Old recipes tend to be for very large quantities, which is discouraging, but spicing can be done just as easily for an ordinary family-sized joint like the one below. Another worry could be that the spicing mixture includes the preservative saltpetre, often reckoned to be a health hazard. However, such a tiny quantity is unlikely to do any harm and people have been preserving meat in this way for generations without any ill-effects, so my advice is don't worry about it.

Although spiced beef can be served hot or cold, I think it is far superior cold, very thinly sliced and served with homemade bread.

4 pounds lean tip roast
¾ cup salt
½ cup brown sugar
1 teaspoon saltpeter (available from the pharmacist)
About 1 quart cold water
1 tablespoon coarsely ground black pepper
1 tablespoon juniper berries, crushed
2 teaspoons ground ginger
1 tablespoon ground cloves
1 teaspoon grated nutmeg
2 teaspoons ground mace
1 tablespoon allspice
1 teaspoon chopped fresh thyme
2 bay leaves, crushed
1 small onion, finely chopped
1 cup Guinness

Place the beef into a good-sized saucepan. Add the salt, brown sugar, saltpetre and water, bring to a boil and boil steadily for 10 minutes. Allow to cool. Then transfer the meat and liquid to a suitable container and keep it in the refrigerator for 5–6 days, turning each day.

Remove the meat from the pickling liquid and drain, discarding the liquid. In a bowl, mix the spices, thyme, bay leaves and onion together. Rub the mixture into the meat and return to the refrigerator for 3–4 days, turning and rubbing daily.

To cook the spiced beef, put the meat into a saucepan and barely cover with cold water. Cover the pan tightly and bring to the boil, then reduce the heat and cook very gently for about 3½ hours. For the last hour, add the Guinness to the cooking liquid. When the meat is cooked, allow it to cool in the liquid. Drain, wrap in foil and keep in the refrigerator until required. It will keep for about a week.

Serves 8.

VARIATION

Spiced tongue: Make spiced tongue in much the same way as beef. For a 4-pound tongue, pickle as for the beef but lighten the spicing mixture by omitting the juniper berries and reducing the other spices by at least half. Spice and cook as for beef, but omit the Guinness. Place the cooked tongue on a board and remove the skin from the tip toward the thicker end, discarding the gristle and bones. Wind into a 6 or 7-inch cake pan or soufflé dish that the meat just fits into. Let set under a weight.

POULTRY

Every Irish countrywoman used to keep fowl — hens, ducks, geese, turkeys and sometimes guinea fowl. Not only did they provide meat and eggs for the household but they were also a source of independent income for her, as any money earned from the sale of poultry or eggs was rightfully hers. Little girls helped their mothers and usually had one or two hens of their own to look after, so they could take a little basket of eggs to market and sell them for pocket money. Until the middle of the nineteenth century pigeons were often kept too, although the ones eaten now are all wild. Wild game has always been plentiful in Ireland.

—————◆ *Chicken and Ham Pie* ◆—————

This tasty pie is worth making from scratch for a large number (the quantities given serve at least 8), but it is not a dish to make on the spur of the moment as the fowl or chicken is best left for several hours (or overnight) to cool in its cooking liquid, if possible. However, you could easily adapt it to make a quick version using leftover chicken and ham.

1 quantity Shortcrust Pastry (see page 110)
1 stewing hen or chicken, about 3½–4 pounds
1½ pounds piece collar or similar boiling bacon, soaked
A few sprigs parsley and thyme, tied together
1 onion or leek, roughly sliced
1 carrot, roughly sliced
Sea salt and freshly ground black pepper
1 onion
8 ounces (about 2⅔ cups) button mushrooms
6 tablespoons (¾ stick) butter
½ cup flour
1 tablespoon freshly chopped parsley
1 egg yolk mixed with 1 tablespoon water to glaze

First make the pastry and set it aside to rest. Put the hen or chicken into a large pan with the bacon, herbs, onion or leek, and carrot. Cover with cold water, season with salt and pepper, and bring to the boil over a moderate heat. Turn down to a simmer and cook until tender — if a chicken is used this won't take much more than an hour, while a hen needs 2½–3 hours. You can remove and set aside the bacon if it shows signs of breaking up, but leave the cooked bird to cool in its cooking liquid, if you can.

When you are ready to assemble the pie, peel and chop the onion and wipe and trim the mushrooms; leave them whole if they are small, otherwise halve or quarter them. Melt 2 tablespoons of the butter in a pan and sweat the onion in it, then add the mushrooms and cook gently until just softened.

Skin the boiling bacon, trim off excess fat and remove any bone or gristle. Cut the bacon into bite-sized chunks. When the chicken or hen is cool, remove from the pan, drain, then remove the skin. Take the flesh off the bones and cut it into manageable pieces. Degrease the cooking liquid by spooning off all the visible fat from the surface, then strain off 2 cups for the sauce. Add the remaining 4 tablespoons butter to the onion and mushrooms, sprinkle in the flour and cook over moderate heat for a minute or two, then gradually stir in the reserved liquid to make a thick sauce. Bring to the boil and cook for a couple of minutes, stirring, then season to taste and add the chopped parsley. Mix the chicken and bacon pieces into the sauce gently but thoroughly; adjust the sauce with a little extra stock if it seems too thick, check the seasoning and turn the mixture into a large deep pie dish (about 2-quart capacity).

On a floured work surface, roll out the pastry to a circle slightly bigger than the pie dish, then trim down to size. Dampen the rim of the pie dish and line with the pastry trimmings, then dampen the pastry rim before covering with the pastry lid. Trim the edges and seal. Cut a hole in the middle of the pie to allow steam to escape and brush the pastry with the beaten egg. Roll out the trimmings and use to make leaves to decorate the middle of the pie. Brush the leaves with egg. Put the pie into a preheated very hot oven (425°F) and cook for 25–30 minutes until the pie is thoroughly heated and the pastry golden brown and crisp. Serve with carrots and a green vegetable.

Serves 8.

Hen in a Pot
⎯⎯⎯◆ *with Parsley Sauce* ◆⎯⎯⎯

Most country people used to have a few hens scratching around, and as they didn't want to lose birds that were still laying eggs it was usually the mature ones that were destined for the pot — and cooking methods that would make the best of bigger birds, with their robust flavor and tougher flesh. A boiling fowl will feed a family both cheaply and well, as this typical country dish demonstrates. A small ham or bacon might also be added to the pot if available: Poultry and ham make good partners at any time and the combination has always been especially relevant in Ireland, where pigs and poultry were the most accessible meats for a large section of the population.

3½–4 pound stewing hen
½ lemon, sliced
A few sprigs of parsley and thyme, tied together

Sea salt and freshly ground black pepper
1½ pounds carrots
6–12 small onions, depending on size
4 tablespoons (½ stick) butter
½ cup flour
1 tablespoon lemon juice
¼ cup finely chopped parsley, plus extra sprigs to garnish
½ cup milk

Place the hen into a large saucepan with enough water to cover and add the sliced lemon, herbs and a seasoning of salt and pepper. Cover and bring to a boil; then reduce the heat and simmer gently for 2½ hours, turning several times during cooking, Meanwhile, scrape the carrots and cut them into large chunks; peel the onions and leave them whole. Add the prepared vegetables to the pot and cook for another 30–35 minutes, until the bird and the vegetables are tender. Using a slotted spoon, lift the fowl onto a warmed serving dish, arrange the vegetables around it and keep warm.

Remove the herbs and lemon slices from the cooking liquid and discard. Bring the liquid back up to a boil and cook rapidly, uncovered, until it has reduced by about one third. Strain and let settle a couple of minutes, then skim the fat off the surface. Melt the butter in a saucepan, add the flour and cook, stirring, for 1 minute. Gradually stir in the chicken stock (there should be about 2 cups) and bring to the boil. Add the lemon juice, parsley and the milk. Taste for seasoning and add a little more salt and a grinding of black pepper, if necessary. Simmer the sauce for another minute or two, then pour a little of it over the hen and the vegetables, and garnish with a few sprigs of fresh parsley. Pour the rest of the sauce into a heated gravy boat. Serve with potatoes boiled or steamed in their jackets and lightly cooked cabbage.

Serves 6.

VARIATION

If you are including a slab of bacon, soak in cold water overnight before cooking and be careful not to add any salt without tasting first. A stewing hen with a 2–2½ pound joint of bacon should give 8–10 servings. Red cabbage is especially good served with the bacon.

◆ *Jellied Chicken* ◆

This old-fashioned dish or "mould" was extremely popular in the nineteenth century. It is a very presentable way of using up bits of chicken that are no longer fit for the table and it is ideal for dealing with the last of the Christmas turkey and ham.

> 2 cups Chicken Stock (see page 107)
> 1½ packets unflavored gelatin
> 2 tablespoons cider vinegar or lemon juice (optional)
> ¾ cup fresh very young peas or cooked peas
> 2 hard-boiled eggs, sliced
> 1 tablespoon freshly chopped parsley
> About 8 ounces cooked chicken or chicken and ham
> Tomatoes, lettuce hearts and cucumber to garnish

Strain off all the fat from the chicken stock. Soak the gelatin in half the stock for 10 minutes, then warm gently until dissolved. Mix with the rest of the stock and the cider vinegar or lemon juice, if using. Rinse a 1-quart soufflé dish (preferably glass) with cold water and drain. Cover the bottom with some of the liquid, chill until set (it won't take long as the quantity is very small), then decorate the layer of set jelly with a row of peas around the edge and sliced hard-boiled eggs in the middle. Scatter in between with chopped parsley and add enough stock to cover. Chill again until firm. Meanwhile, either finely chop the chicken (and ham, if using) or mince it. Warm the remaining stock gently to a liquid if it has thickened too much, then add the chopped chicken, the rest of the peas and chop and add the remaining hard-boiled eggs. Mix well. When cold and beginning to thicken, pour it into the mold. Chill until set, then turn out onto a serving dish and garnish with tomatoes, lettuce hearts and cucumber.

Serves 4.

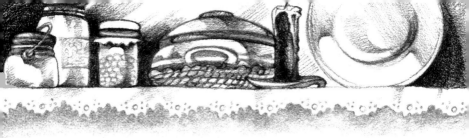

5. Vegetables

The wonderful walled gardens of the great country houses were well known for the abundance and variety of their produce, but every Irish farmhouse also used to have its kitchen garden. The main crops were potato and cabbage, with a number of varieties of each grown to give different cooking and eating qualities as well as extend the season as much as possible. A typical country garden would also supply the family with white and yellow turnips, carrots and parsnips, onions and leeks. Greens such as Brussels sprouts, broccoli, cauliflowers, runner beans and peas were all widely grown, and more adventurous gardeners also made time for treats such as asparagus and even crops that needed to be grown under glass, such as cucumbers and tomatoes. A spot handy to the back door was always reserved for herbs — parsley, thyme, sage and chives, of course, a few bulbs of garlic, and bushes of aromatics such as bay, rosemary and lavender.

⟶ ✦*Jerusalem Artichokes* ✦ ⟵

Jerusalem artichokes are very easy to grow and old recipes show that they used to be popular. Newer varieties are less knobbly than the older ones and therefore are much easier to prepare. Jerusalem artichokes have a very subtle flavor and very white, almost translucent flesh, which is totally unlike the floury potato. The cooking liquid cools to make a delicious jellied stock. They are most often used in a very good soup with a sophisticated flavor that makes it a favorite in the more adventurous country restaurants and for dinner parties, but they deserve to be served more often as a vegetable in their own right. They are very good served in the traditional way in a white sauce — I always do them like this on Christmas Day.

> 1½ pounds Jerusalem artichokes
> Lemon juice or vinegar
> Good knob of butter
> Sea salt and freshly ground black pepper
> 2 cups White Sauce (see page 108) made with
>   artichoke cooking liquid

Peel the artichokes and put them straight into a bowl of water acidulated with a dash of lemon juice or vinegar to prevent discoloration. Cut them, if necessary, so they will cook evenly, otherwise the larger ones will still be hard in the middle when the small ones start to disintegrate. Put into a pan containing enough boiling, salted water to cover and add a good squeeze of lemon juice or vinegar to keep them white. Bring back to the boil, then reduce the heat and simmer for about 15–20 minutes or until they are just tender. Watch them carefully as they start to break up very suddenly. Drain the cooking liquid off into a jug, then add a knob of butter and a light seasoning of salt and freshly ground black pepper to the pan, turn the artichokes in the melting butter, then put in a heated serving dish and keep warm. Make the white sauce using 1 cup heavy cream and 1 cup reserved artichoke stock. Coat the artichokes with the sauce and serve as soon as possible.

Serves 6.

VARIATION

Cook the artichokes as above, then remove from the pan with a slotted spoon and allow to cool. Chill and serve with basic oil and vinegar dressing, garnished with freshly chopped parsley.

➤ *Beets with Lemon Dressing* ◆—

1 pound evenly sized beets
Grated rind and juice of ½ small lemon
Scant ½ cup olive and sunflower oil, mixed
Sea salt and freshly ground black pepper
Freshly chopped parsley or chives (optional)

Cook the beets in boiling salted water for about half an hour until tender — test by pinching the skin between two fingers: If it comes away easily the beets are cooked. Drain and, when cool enough to handle, peel and slice into a bowl. Add the lemon rind and juice, oil and seasoning to taste. Mix gently and let the beets cool completely in the dressing. Scatter with chopped herbs before serving, if you like.

Serves 4.

VARIATIONS

Yogurt, lightly flavored with lemon rind and juice and seasoned with salt and pepper, also goes very well with beets and makes a pretty pink sauce as the beet juice blends into it.

———————◆ *Red Cabbage* ◆———————

Second only to the potato, cabbage is the most widely grown and commonly eaten vegetable in Ireland. Red cabbage is especially valuable as it is the only brassica which you can cook ahead (and even reheat) without spoiling. The flavor and texture of red cabbage is robust and it complements other hearty foods, such as ham, beef and game. Unfortunately, presumably for reasons of convenience, many restaurants insist on serving it with fish, which makes a disastrous combination. Make this popular version on top of the stove or in the oven.

> 1 onion
> oil
> 1 small red cabbage
> 2 cooking apples
> 1 tablespoon red currant jelly (see page 111)
> 2 tablespoons cider vinegar
> Sea salt and freshly ground black pepper
> 3–4 crushed allspice berries

Peel and chop the onion. Heat the oil in a wide-based cast-iron casserole and cook the onion gently in it for about 5 minutes until softened. Meanwhile, shred the red cabbage and peel and slice the apples. Stir all the remaining ingredients into the onion and bring to a boil. Keep stirring until the red currant jelly dissolves. Cover and simmer gently or cook in a moderate oven (350°F) for about 45 minutes or until the cabbage is tender. Check the seasoning before serving. Reserve some, if you can, as it makes a good cold accompaniment to leftover meat.

Serves 6–8.

—◆ *Dry-Panned Mushrooms* ◆—

Wild field mushrooms are at their best in late summer and early autumn, when they are there for the picking all over the country — if you're an early riser anyway. This is Florence Irwin's traditional way of cooking them:

Make a small, thin frying pan very hot. Have some nice, well-developed mushrooms about 2–3 inches in diameter. Peel and remove the stems. Place them in the hot frying pan, with the gills on top; on each one put a piece of butter the size of a hazelnut, and a pinch of salt. Keep over a good heat until the butter begins to boil and the mushrooms are cooked. Serve on good well-buttered toast. Delicious!

◆ *Baked Parsnips* ◆

Parsnips are a popular garden crop in areas where the soil is suitable and they have been in use since early times. Like potatoes, parsnips respond well to a variety of cooking methods — they can be cut to the same size as the potatoes and roasted with them around the joint, they can be boiled, puréed, fried or made into cakes like potato cakes. However, this simple method delivers them to the table tender and ready-buttered, and beats them all. In winter, I often bake parsnips like this when doing a roast.

> 4 evenly sized, small-to-medium parsnips
> 4 sheets generously buttered parchment paper
> Sea salt and freshly ground black pepper
> Heavy brown paper

Wash and trim the parsnips. Remove the core at the top with a small knife and cut a deep cross into the thickest part to help them cook evenly. Lay each one on a buttered parchment, season with salt and pepper if you wish, and roll up tightly to make a neat package. Roll again in a layer of heavy brown paper and put the parsnips in a moderate oven (350°F). Bake for 1–1½ hours, or until the parsnips feel soft when squeezed. You can adjust the temperature and timing to suit other dishes in the oven. Remove the parsnips from the papers just before serving with the buttery juices poured over.

Serves 4.

Potatoes Boiled in Their Jackets

This was the traditional method of cooking potatoes and is still the most popular today. People living by the sea preferred to boil them in sea water because the salt content prevented the skins from cracking and none of the mineral content was lost. For boiling in their jackets, potatoes must be "floury," as no amount of cooking will make a "soapy" one nice. As a rule red potatoes are more floury than white ones.

Potatoes
Salt
Water

To boil new potatoes:

Have enough boiling water to cover the potatoes. Salt it. Wash the potatoes and put into the boiling salted water. Bring quickly to a boil. Boil steadily until tender. Drain at once. After draining, place a clean cloth on top of the potatoes and place on the stove to "dry" them. A few minutes suffice for this process. Serve at once.

To boil old potatoes:

Wash well. When they start to sprout, slice off and discard the growing part. Place in a saucepan. Cover with cold water. Add enough salt to make the water decidedly salty. Cover. Bring to the boil. Boil steadily till tender. Drain at once. "Dry" them by placing a towel on top for a few minutes. Serve at once.

To peel: Put on a side plate, skin with a knife and fork, then lift onto the dinner plate.

Champ

Champ is a well-loved dish in the north of Ireland, where it always used to be a favorite Friday dinner. That marvelous northern Irish

cookery expert Florence Irwin described champ in *The Cookin'
Woman* as it used to be, a real country dish:

> In a farmhouse two stones or more of potatoes were peeled and
> boiled for the dinner. Then the man of the house was sum-
> moned when all was ready, and while he pounded this enor-
> mous potful of potatoes with a sturdy wooden beetle his wife
> added the potful of milk and nettles, or scallions, or chives, or
> parsley, and he beetled it until it was smooth as butter, not a
> lump anywhere. Everyone got a large bowlful, made a hole in
> the center, and into this put a large lump of butter. Then the
> champ was eaten from the outside with a spoon or fork,
> dipping it into the melting butter in the center. All was washed
> down with new milk or freshly churned buttermilk.

The flavoring in champ could be freshly chopped chives or parsley,
chopped nettle tops (which were boiled with the milk for 20 minutes), or onions or scallions (spring onions). The chopped onions
might be scalded first to make them more digestible, or simply
boiled with the milk like nettle tops.

This is the basic recipe, using chives:

> 1½ pounds potatoes
> ½ cup freshly chopped chives, or more, to taste
> About 1 cup milk
> Sea salt and freshly ground black pepper
> Butter to serve

Peel the potatoes and boil in salted water until tender. Meanwhile,
boil the chives for 5 minutes in the milk — this is optional, as many
people like the chives raw, in which case just heat the milk. Drain the
potatoes when they are ready, cover with a clean cloth and "dry" over
low heat for a few minutes. Then mash by whatever method you
normally use. When free from lumps, beat in the boiling milk and
chives. Working over the heat so that the champ is kept very hot, beat
until the consistency is very creamy. Season well with black pepper
and plenty of salt. Use more milk if necessary. Serve as described
above, on hot plates.

Serves 2–3 as a main dish, 4–6 as a side dish or part of a selection.

◆ *Colcannon* ◆

A great Halloween specialty, colcannon was traditionally made with curly kale although cabbage is more often used now. Halloween has more traditional festive dishes associated with it than any other day in the Irish calendar and, because it is actually a fast day, they are all vegetarian. Barm brack is popular throughout Ireland, but other specialties vary from region to region. Whichever dish is chosen, a ring is put into it that will predict a marriage in the coming year for the person who finds it on his or her plate. This traditional rhyme almost gives the recipe for colcannon:

> *Did you ever eat colcannon*
> *When 'twas made of thickened cream,*
> *And the greens and scallions blended*
> *Like pictures in a dream?*
>
> *Did you ever scoop a hole on top*
> *To hold the melting cake*
> *Of clover-flavored butter*
> *Which your mother used to make?*
>
> *Did you ever eat and eat, afraid*
> *You'd let the ring go past,*
> *And like some old married "sprissman"*
> *Would get it at the last?*

1 bowl mashed potatoes
1 bowl cooked cabbage or curly kale, chopped
1 onion
2 tablespoons dripping per pound vegetables
Sea salt and freshly ground black pepper to taste
Milk if necessary
1 ring, wrapped in parchment paper

Combine the mashed potatoes and the cabbage or kale. Mix well. Peel and chop the onion. Melt a little of the dripping in a large, heavy frying pan or griddle and cook the onion in it. Remove and mix with the potato and cabbage. Season to taste, and stir in a little milk if the mixture is too stiff. Add the rest of the dripping to the hot pan and, when very hot, turn the potato and cabbage into the pan and spread it out. Fry until golden, then roughly cut it and continue frying until there are lots of crisp brown pieces. Just before serving, slip in the wrapped ring—the trick, as you can see from the rhyme, is to make sure the ring doesn't turn up too soon; then the children will eat it all willingly!

◆ Swiss Chard ◆

You'll find Swiss chard (called Spinach Beet in Ireland) a good crop. If you grow your own vegetables, it bolts much less easily than ordinary spinach and it makes two meals. The first day you cook only the leaves and serve in the same way as spinach; the next day you cook the stalks like asparagus and serve with a little cream or a white sauce. Or you can serve both together, with the green leaves heaped up in the middle of a serving dish and the stems arranged around them.

    2 pounds Swiss chard
    1 tablespoon butter
    A little grated nutmeg
    Lemon juice
    White Sauce (see page 108) or 2 tablespoons heavy cream
    Sea salt and freshly ground black pepper

To cook the leaves:
Remove the stalks. Wash the leaves well and lift straight into a lightly greased heavy-bottomed saucepan. The water clinging to the leaves will be enough so don't add any more. Cover with a tight-fitting lid and cook over moderate heat for about 5 minutes, shaking the pan occasionally. Drain well, then add the butter and nutmeg. When the butter has melted, toss it all together and serve immediately.

To cook the stalks:
Trim the base of the stalks, wash well and tie in bundles like asparagus. Add to a pan containing boiling water, with a good

squeeze of lemon juice added, and cook for about 20 minutes until tender. Drain and serve coated with white sauce or simply add the cream, heat through gently, season with salt and pepper, and serve.

Serves 4.

VARIATION
Chop the cooked leaves finely and gently reheat in the pan with ½ cup heavy cream. Season with freshly ground black pepper and serve immediately.

Zucchini and Cauliflower Cheese

This makes a good vegetable accompaniment and can also be served as a light meal if ham is included. You can use other vegetables, such as celery or carrots, instead of the zucchini.

    1 pound zucchini
    1 medium cauliflower
    Cheese Sauce made with 1 cup milk (see page 109)
    2–4 ounces mixed Cheddar and Romano cheese, grated
    8 ounces lean cooked ham (optional)

Wipe and trim the zucchini and, unless they are very small, cut them up into 1-inch pieces. Trim the cauliflower and cut it up into florets. Put both vegetables into a little salted boiling water in a large pan and cook for about 10 minutes or until just tender. Drain the cooked vegetables, turn into a shallow buttered gratin dish, pour over the sauce and sprinkle with the grated cheese. Put under the broiler or in a hot oven for a few minutes to brown. If including the ham, dice it and mix in with the vegetables before adding the sauce.

Serves 4.

6. Desserts

The best Irish desserts and puddings are homey, comforting dishes — filling, certainly, but based on healthy country ingredients. Every farmhouse used to have its orchard where you would always find apples and often pears, cherries and plums. Fruit, both wild and cultivated, has always played an important role in the Irish kitchen. Apples, especially, are highly valued and have been grown in Ireland for over a thousand years. They are connected to many folk customs, especially at Halloween when traditional games like bobbing for apples are still played, and as they are then at the height of their season they are an ingredient in many of the traditional Halloween dishes. "Cottage-garden" fruits, such as black currants, raspberries and, especially, gooseberries and rhubarb, for example, have all been used freely down through the generations. Hazelnuts, too, are to be found in the wild in some areas and walnuts were once quite common, although they virtually disappeared during the wars of the nineteenth century because walnut wood was

used to make guns. Almonds, on the other hand, although a favorite ingredient in old Irish recipes, especially from the eighteenth century, would have been imported. Honey was used for sweetening from earliest times and, although sugar has been in general use for hundreds of years now, many dishes still exist that depend on the special, aromatic flavor of honey.

The other major influence in the development of desserts was, of course, milk. A very high proportion of traditional desserts were milk puddings of one kind or another, often made with oatmeal, barley or, from the mid-nineteenth century, rice. On most farms, cream was used mainly to make butter for sale, so richer dishes containing cream would have been made mostly in the kitchens of the "big houses" or in the more prosperous farmhouses for special occasions. A high proportion of cream in a dish is often a sign that the recipe is modern or, like the one that follows, adapted to suit the tastes of a more prosperous age.

Mr. Guinness's
━━━━━━ ◆ *Christmas Pudding* ◆ ━━━━━━

The custom of serving a rich plum pudding at Christmas is not very old, but a simpler boiled pudding on similar lines was traditional in some areas. Folk historian Kevin Danaher says that in Co. Wexford, for example, "Cutlin Pudding was made on Christmas Eve: first a thick porridge of wheaten meal was prepared, then sugar, dried fruit and spices were added and the whole was made into a ball as big as, or bigger than, a football, and wrapped in a greased cloth ready for boiling" (*The Year in Ireland*, The Mercier Press, 1972).

After being introduced to the kitchens of big houses in Victorian times, the rich pudding we know today very quickly became established as a Christmas tradition. This is a modernized version from "Uncle Arthur," as the Guinness brewery is affectionately known in Dublin. Guinness makes a flavorsome contribution to a wide variety of dishes, notably game and red meat or any with a high dried-fruit content. Unlike their simpler predecessors, rich Christmas puddings need to be made at least a month before use to allow them to mature; if properly stored, they will keep until the following Christmas.

> 5 cups fresh whole-wheat bread crumbs
> 1 cup dark brown sugar
> 1¾ cups currants
> 1¾ cups raisins, chopped
> 1¾ cups golden raisins
> 2 ounces chopped mixed peel
> 10 ounces shredded suet
> ½ level teaspoon salt
> 2–4 teaspoons pumpkin pie spice
> Grated rind of 1 lemon
> 2 teaspoons lemon juice
> 2 large eggs, beaten
> ½ cup skimmed or low-fat milk
> 1 cup Guinness Extra

Mix all the dry ingredients in a large basin. Stir in the lemon juice, eggs, milk and Guinness. Mix well and turn into two 2½ pint/1.5 liter pudding basins, well greased and base-lined. Tie pudding cloths over the puddings, or cover them tightly with several layers of greased greaseproof paper and foil. Leave overnight, then steam for about 7½ hours (make sure they do not go off the boil, and top up with more boiling water as necessary). When cool, re-cover the puddings and store in a cool, dry place. When required, steam for another 2–3 hours and serve with Whiskey Sauce (see page 109) or any of the other recommended sauces.

Makes 2 puddings, each serving 6–8.

⬩ *Apple Snow* ⬩

Thinking of apple snow brings back nostalgic memories of tea with a favorite aunt in her tiny cottage, called "The Nest" because it was almost part of a rookery. We used to have boiled farmyard eggs with "soldiers" and apple snow with cookies crumbled on top. Heaven.

> 1½ pounds cooking apples
> 3 tablespoons water
> 2 pieces thinly peeled lemon rind (optional)
> ½ cup sugar
> 3 egg whites

Peel and core the apples, slice into a saucepan and add the water and lemon rind, if using. Cover and simmer gently until the apples "fall" — about 15 minutes. Remove from the heat, remove the lemon rind and mix in the sugar. Make a purée by mixing in a blender, putting through a food mill or rubbing through a sieve. Set aside until cool.

Whisk the egg whites until stiff, then carefully fold into the purée with a metal spoon. Put into glass serving dishes and chill. Serve with brown sugar and whipped cream — or, of course, with crumbled cookies.

Serves 6.

Blackberry and Apple Crumble

This is another old favorite. The oatmeal in the topping makes this traditional hot pudding especially crunchy and delicious.

2 pounds cooking apples
1 pound blackberries
2 tablespoons water
¼ cup granulated sugar
8 tablespoons (1 stick) butter
1 cup whole-wheat flour
⅔ cup oatmeal
¼ cup brown sugar

Peel, core and slice the cooking apples. Wash the blackberries and pick over them. Put the fruit, water and granulated sugar into a large shallow ovenproof dish, about 4-quart capacity.

To make the crumble topping, rub the butter into the flour, then add the oatmeal and brown sugar and continue to rub in until the mixture begins to stick together, like big crumbs. Use to cover the fruit, packing down lightly. Bake in a preheated hot oven (400°F) for 15 minutes, then reduce the heat to 375°F and cook for another 15–20 minutes until cooked through and crunchy brown on top. Serve very hot with whipped cream or ice cream.

Serves 6–8.

→ *Bread and Butter Pudding* ←

Comfort food of the highest order, this is a nursery favorite. This version was given to me by Feargal O'hUiginn of Oisíns.

> 8 slices white bread, buttered
> 1 cup golden raisins and dark raisins mixed
> ½ teaspoon freshly grated nutmeg
> A little sugar
> 2 eggs
> Scant 1 cup heavy cream
> Scant 2 cups milk
> 3–4 drops vanilla extract
> ½ cup sugar
> Brown sugar (optional)

Remove the crusts from the bread and put 4 slices, buttered side down, in the base of an ovenproof dish. Sprinkle with the mixed dried fruit, half the nutmeg and a pinch of sugar. Place the remaining 4 slices of bread on top, buttered side down, and sprinkle again with nutmeg and sugar. Lightly beat the eggs, add the cream, milk, vanilla and sugar, then mix well to make a custard. Pour this mixture over the bread, sprinkle a little brown or additional white sugar over the top if you like to have a crisp crust, and bake in a preheated moderate oven (350°F) for 1 hour or until all the liquid has been absorbed and the pudding is well risen and golden brown. Serve with whipped cream or a scoop of vanilla ice cream — the contrast between the hot and cold is delicious!

Serves 6.

⟶ *Irish Coffee Cake* ←

This gooey cake is made in a ring shape, which makes it much easier to serve.

8 tablespoons (1 stick) butter, at room temperature
½ cup sugar
2 eggs
1 cup self-rising flour
1–2 tablespoons coffee extract

Irish coffee syrup:

½ cup strong black coffee
½ cup sugar
¼ cup Irish whiskey

To decorate:

½ cup heavy cream
Confectioners' sugar to taste
1 tablespoon whiskey, or to taste
Chopped nuts or grated chocolate

Grease and flour an 8-inch ring cake pan. Preheat a moderate oven (350°F). Cream the butter and sugar until light and fluffy, then beat in the eggs, adding a little flour at a time and beating well after each addition. Stir in the coffee extract and mix thoroughly. Turn the mixture into the prepared pan and bake for 35–40 minutes until springy to the touch. Turn out and cool on a wire rack.

IRISH COFFEE SYRUP

To make the Irish coffee syrup, put the coffee and sugar into a small pan and bring up to a boil, stirring to dissolve the sugar, then boil for 1 minute. Remove from the heat and add the whiskey.

Wash and dry the pan the cake was baked in and return the cooled cake to it, then pour the hot coffee syrup all over it. Leave in a cool place for several hours, then turn out. Whip the cream until it is thick, sweeten lightly with confectioners' sugar and add whiskey to taste. Spread the cake with the whipped cream and chill for an hour before serving sprinkled with chopped nuts or grated chocolate.

Makes 1 8-inch ring cake.

⸻ ✦ *Irish Whiskey Trifle* ✦ ⸻

A well-made trifle is a mouthwateringly wicked treat, often associated with Christmas. This one is made with homemade sponge cake, fresh fruit and rich egg custard. Don't take shortcuts with the custard — that's the crucial ingredient.

Custard:

> 1½ cups whole milk
> 1 vanilla pod or a few drops of vanilla extract
> 3 eggs
> 2 tablespoons sugar
>
> 1 small sponge cake made with 2 eggs (see page 102)
> Raspberry jam
> ½ cup whiskey
> 1 pound fruit, e.g., pears and bananas
> Lemon juice (optional)
> 1 cup heavy cream
> Blanched almonds, glacé cherries and angelica to
>   decorate (optional)

First make the custard. Put the milk into a pan with the vanilla pod (split open, if you use it), and bring almost to a boil. Remove from the heat. Whisk the eggs and sugar together lightly in a bowl. Remove the vanilla pod from the pan and set aside to wash and re-use. Gradually whisk the milk into the egg mixture. Rinse out the pan with cold water, return the mixture to it and stir over a very low heat until it thickens. Do not allow it to boil. (It's a good idea to keep a big bowl of cold water handy — if the custard shows signs of curdling, plunge the pan into the water and stir, which will bring the temperature down very quickly. Alternatively, use a double-boiler or a bowl set over — but not touching — boiling water, if making custards makes you nervous.) Turn the custard into a bowl and set aside, stirring occasionally to prevent a skin forming. If using vanilla extract, stir it in now.

Halve the sponge cake horizontally, spread with raspberry jam and make a sandwich. Cut into slices and use them to line the bottom and the lower sides of a large glass dessert bowl. Sprinkle generously with the whiskey. Peel and slice the fruit, sprinkle with lemon juice or whiskey to prevent discoloration, then spread it out over the sponge to make an even layer. Strain the custard on top, cover with a plate and leave to cool. Chill.

Before serving, whip the cream and spread it over the custard, then decorate with the traditional blanched split almonds, glacé cherries and angelica if you like.

Serves 6–8.

——→ *Potato Apple Dumpling* ◆——

This old-fashioned pudding, made with a potato paste and boiled in a cloth, was traditional at Halloween in some parts of the country, when it would include a ring wrapped in wax paper — whoever got the ring would be married within the year. This version is from Florence Irwin's remarkable book *The Cookin' Woman*, published in 1949. Quantities given are flexible, as in many country recipes, to allow for varying availability of ingredients.

> 1 bowlful boiled and riced potatoes, still warm
> About 4 tablespoons (½ stick) butter (2 tablespoons if
>   dumpling is small)
> Pinch of ground ginger
> Enough flour to make a paste
> Salt

Apple filling:

> Apples
> Cloves
> Sugar

Topping:

> Butter
> Lemon juice
> Pinch of nutmeg

You will need a square cloth. This may be of strong unbleached calico — a portion of a flour bag is quite adequate. To prepare, have it well washed and boil it for 10 minutes without either soap or soda, then wring it out. (If the cloth has been used for puddings before and is kept for that purpose only, all you need to do is scald it in boiling water.) Then dredge it thickly with flour. This forms a coat when it is put on to boil and prevents the water boiling into the pastry. Have on the stove a pot of fast-boiling water. Put an old plate into the pot for the pudding to rest on. Peel and core the apples; cut into small pieces.

To make the pastry: Flour a board and place the mashed potatoes on it. Melt the butter and pour it evenly over them, adding a good pinch of ground ginger and enough salt to season. Over this, sift some flour and with the hands work it in. Continue adding flour until you get a nice workable dough that can be kneaded and rolled out. Never work in too much flour — you'll only get a tough, hard paste. The less kneading the lighter the paste, but it must be of a consistency to roll out smoothly. Roll it to a round and carefully lift it onto the floured cloth. In the center put the apples, 2 or 3 cloves and enough sugar to sweeten. Damp the edges of the pastry and gather it up on top, sealing well. Tie up in the floured cloth quite firmly, as the apples will shrink in cooking. Have a loop on the string so you can lift the dumpling easily.

To boil: Have the pot "walloping" over a good heat. Drop in the dumpling. Put on the lid tightly. Boil steadily for 1½–2 hours, filling up the pot with boiling water as evaporation takes place.

To dish out: Lift the dumpling from the pot into a colander. Drain for a few moments. Remove the string and carefully turn the dumpling out onto a hot dish. Serve on hot plates, with melted butter seasoned with a little lemon juice and a pinch of nutmeg. For Halloween add a ring well wrapped in wax paper.

—✦ *Rhubarb and Orange Fool* ✦—

Fools can be made with any kind of puréed fruit mixed with whipped cream or egg custard or a mixture of the two, but they seem to be especially successfully made with a sharply flavored cottage-garden produce like rhubarb. The cream or custard takes the hard edge off the fruit, while still leaving enough "bite" to be interesting.

> 1 pound rhubarb
> 1 large orange
> 4 rounded tablespoons clear honey (easier to
>   measure if you heat the spoon first)
> 1 cup heavy cream or thick egg custard
>   or an equal mixture of both
> Whipped cream and peeled orange segments to decorate

Wash the rhubarb, remove and discard the leaves, and cut it into 1-inch pieces. Finely grate the zest from the orange and squeeze the juice. Put the rhubarb into a saucepan with the rind, strained juice and honey, stir over low heat until the honey has melted, then cook gently until the rhubarb is tender. Purée in a blender or through a sieve and let cool.

If using cream, whip it until thick. Using a metal spoon, fold the whipped cream and/or custard gently but thoroughly into the fruit. Put into serving glasses and chill. Decorate with some extra whipped cream and peeled orange segments and serve with crisp biscuits.

Serves 4–6.

VARIATION
Add a dash of an orange-flavored liqueur.

⟶• *Rhubarb Layer Cake* •⟶

This is a personal favorite of mine and can be made with all kinds of fruit, including blackberry and apple, but I especially like the contrast between the sweet layers and really tart fruit such as green gooseberries or rhubarb. Rhubarb is not really a fruit at all but like tomatoes (which are) has earned its place by common usage. This cake is best made with flour for the base and a mixture of flour and oatmeal for the topping.

> 1–1½ pounds rhubarb

Topping:

> ¾ cup self-rising flour
> ⅓ cup oatmeal
> ⅓ cup brown sugar
> 6 tablespoons (¾ stick) butter
> 1 tablespoon water

Base:

> 6 ounces self-rising whole-wheat flour
> 8 tablespoons (1 stick) butter
> ½ cup brown sugar
> 2 large eggs
> Few drops vanilla extract
> A little milk to mix

Trim the rhubarb, discarding all the leaves, wash and dry, then slice fairly finely. To make the crumble topping, mix the flour, oatmeal and sugar in a bowl, then cut in the butter and rub in until fine and crumbly. Set aside while you make the base. Sift the flour. Cream the butter and sugar until light and fluffy. Mix the eggs and vanilla lightly together, then gradually beat into the creamed mixture, adding a little of the flour each time with the egg. Add the remaining flour and mix in gently, adding enough milk to keep the consistency fairly soft.

Grease the base and sides of an 8–9 inch deep tart or springform pan. Spread the base mixture evenly in the bottom of the pan and cover it with the prepared rhubarb. Add the tablespoon of water to the prepared crumble mixture and stir so that it forms larger lumps.

Sprinkle the topping over the rhubarb, spreading evenly with the back of a fork. Bake in a preheated moderate oven (350°F) for about 1 hour or until the rhubarb is tender and the crumble topping crisp and golden brown. Let the cake cool and firm up a little before removing it from the pan. It is probably most delicious sprinkled with a little granulated or confectioners' sugar and served warm with whipped cream or ice cream as a dessert, but it also makes an unusual addition to the tea table, served cold as a cake.

Serves 6–8.

VARIATION

Cherry Cake: Substitute 1–1½ pounds cherries (pitted weight) for the rhubarb. For the topping, use 1 cup self-rising flour instead of the flour and oatmeal, and substitute white sugar for the brown. Similarly, use white flour and sugar instead of the whole-wheat flour and brown sugar in the base mixture.

✦ *Rice Pudding* ✦

A good rice pudding is cooked slowly, producing a creamy layer of rice covered with a delicious thin brown skin. This was a favorite of my father in his farming days. We sometimes used to add 1 oz/25g sultanas with the rice.

> 1 tablespoon butter
> ⅓ cup Carolina rice
> Pinch of salt
> 2 cups whole milk
> 1 tablespoon sugar

Use the butter to grease a shallow pie dish. Wash and drain the rice and put it into the dish with the salt, milk and sugar. Bake in a preheated slow oven (300°F) for 2 hours or until the rice is tender. Stir it occasionally until the milk is hot and the grains start to burst.

When ready, the top will be a lovely deep golden brown and the rice underneath will be creamy.

Serves 4–6.

VARIATION

You can make different milk puddings in the same way using other grains, such as sago or tapioca.

✦ *Summer Pudding* ✦

Although it is a very simple dish, summer pudding is lush and colorful, and somehow always seems to have an air of glamour. You can vary the exact proportions of the fruits to suit what is available.

> 1 loaf white bread, 2–3 days old
> 1½ pounds mixed fruit, e.g., raspberries, strawberries, cherries, etc.
> About ½ cup sugar or 5 tablespoons honey

Remove the crusts from the loaf and thinly slice the bread. Use to line the base and sides of a 1-quart pudding bowl or soufflé dish, cutting the slices so that the pieces fit closely together. Hull the fruit, if necessary, and wash carefully, removing stones (if using cherries, for example). Put the fruit into a wide, heavy-bottomed pan, sprinkle the sugar or honey over and bring very gently to a boil. Cook for 2–3 minutes, or until the juices run. Remove the pan from the heat and set aside 2–3 tablespoons of the juices. Spoon the fruit and remaining juices into the prepared dish and cover the top closely with the remaining slices of bread. Put a plate that neatly fits inside the top of the dish on top of the pudding and weigh it down with a heavy can or jar. Leave in the refrigerator for 8 hours, or overnight. Before serving, remove the weight and plate, cover the bowl with a serving plate and turn upside down to unmold the pudding. Use the reserved fruit juice to pour over any patches of the bread that have not been soaked and colored by the fruit juices. Serve with a bowl of lightly whipped cream.

Serves 6–8.

VARIATION

Autumn Pudding: Make autumn pudding in the same way as summer pudding, but use seasonal fruit such as blackberries and apples instead.

Whiskey and Almond Flummery

A flummery is an old dish that all the Celtic countries have in common, give or take some local variations. A traditional Irish flummery is most often a cooked cold dessert based on oatmeal, although I have old recipes for what is in effect an almond cream under the same name and, at the other extreme, for a sort of hot gruel.

This is a rich, uncooked flummery and, although the ingredients are very much traditional Irish (including the almonds, which were so popular in the eighteenth century), it is much more suited to modern tastes—and much closer to the Highland flummery that Flora MacDonald is said to have been eating when she was arrested in 1746 after helping Bonnie Prince Charlie into hiding on the Isle of Skye. A similar Welsh dish also exists—a good example of the close links between Celtic kitchens.

> ⅓ cup almonds
> 2 ounces McCann's Irish Oatmeal
> 1 cup heavy cream
> 3–4 tablespoons clear clover honey to taste
> ¼ cup whiskey or Irish Mist liqueur
> Juice of ½ lemon

Heat the almonds and oatmeal gently in a heavy-bottomed pan until they turn golden brown, then set aside. Whip the cream until it is smooth but not stiff. Melt the honey slightly so that it runs easily, then fold the honey, whiskey or Irish Mist, half the toasted almonds and oatmeal, and the lemon juice into the cream. Mix lightly but thoroughly, put the warm mixture into tall individual glasses and sprinkle the remaining almonds and oatmeal over the top.

Serves 4–6.

7. Bread and Baking

Bread is one of the great strengths of Irish cooking — in fact it would be easy to fill a book with bread recipes alone, as everyone in Ireland has his or her own variation with its special characteristics. Every self-respecting Irish restaurant makes its own bread, usually to a special recipe which they are delighted to share.

The Irish bread-making tradition is a direct result of the fact that the traditional hearth had no built-in oven. By the time cooking ranges were later installed in the hearth this tradition was so well established that the oven was not used for breadmaking, which was still done on the griddle or in the old-fashioned oven-pot which hung over the fire or rested on a trivet and was known as a bastable. Despite the fact that the modern Irish kitchen is much the same as

any other in Europe, and most people now bake variations of traditional recipes using ordinary bread pans in gas or electric ovens, the traditional method of cooking in the bastable lives on through the practice of making bread in a cast-iron casserole with the lid on. In early times, the traditional unleavened "thin bread" was the oaten farl, shaped like a quarter circle and cooked on a hot flagstone or, later, an iron bakestone. The large circular cake was marked with a cross so that it could easily be broken into quarters (farls) after baking and hardening on a wrought-iron "harnen stand," or toaster, in front of the fire. A modernized form of this cooking method is still sometimes used (see the recipe introduction for Oatcakes on page 90) and the tradition of baking on the griddle also survives; where a griddle isn't practical (on an electric burner, for example), a heavy cast-iron frying pan is often used instead.

Just as the baking technique in Ireland was very different from countries where oven-baking was the norm, so were the ingredients. As might be expected, there is no great tradition of yeast cookery in Ireland. Instead, the leavening agents were buttermilk and bicarbonate of soda (baking soda), which were — and still are — widely used for all kinds of bread, scones and cakes made with wheat, oats or potato and flour mixtures. Maize, or "Indian corn," was mixed in with other flours to make bread in the famine years and was still used in some areas during the first half of this century.

Dr. E. Estyn Evans says in *Irish Folk Ways* that the major disadvantage of unyeasted bread — its poor keeping quality — made the housewife the "slave of the fire":

> Laborers have been known to refuse to work on farms where there was not a daily baking of bread. The baking board or trough hung ready on the wall, and the meal was stored near the fire to keep it dry. Old people have told me how, when they were children, they were called on periodically to tramp the meal in its wooden chest or ark, treading it down with bare feet to drive out the air and lessen the risk of its going musty.

However, despite the "slavery" of the daily baking, soda bread is utterly delicious when freshly eaten and is very quick and easy to mix — which may well explain why such a high proportion of Irish people continue to bake their own bread. Also, as you will notice when you try the recipes in this chapter, many of them (especially the whole-wheat ones) actually keep better than might be expected and certainly make excellent toast after several days.

If you don't have buttermilk on hand, you can use milk soured with a little lemon juice instead. If you don't have bicarbonate of soda, use fresh milk and baking powder instead. Some recipes include cream of tartar (even when buttermilk is used) to increase the acid content and help the dough to rise faster. Don't be tempted to use too much soda, as it will spoil the flavor and white bread will turn a yellowish color. Work quickly and lightly to make light bread, and keep the dough fairly wet, adding more liquid than specified if necessary — the absorbency of flour varies considerably and a dry dough makes heavy bread.

Although the variety and excellence of bread is the basic strength of Irish baking, biscuits, scones and, especially, cakes are also a cause for pride. Irish cooks are great bakers and it always used to be a point of honor to have a good selection on the table for supper.

——◆ *Basic Brown Soda Bread* ◆——

This simple, wholesome bread is best eaten fresh, but slices better if left to cool and "set" for at least 4 hours.

> 3¾ cups coarse whole-wheat flour
> 1½ cups all-purpose flour
> 1 rounded teaspoon baking soda
> 1 teaspoon salt
> About 1½ cups buttermilk

Preheat a hot oven (400°F). Mix the dry ingredients in a bowl and stir in enough buttermilk to make a fairly soft dough. Turn onto a work surface dusted with wholemeal flour and knead lightly until smooth underneath. Form into a circle, about 1½ inches thick, and put on a greased or floured baking sheet. Mark a deep cross in the top with a floured knife. Bake for about 45 minutes, or until the bread is browned and sounds hollow when tapped on the base. Cool on a wire rack, wrapped in a clean linen towel if you want to keep the crust soft.

Makes 1 large loaf.

Traditional ——◆ *White Soda Bread* ◆——

> 4 cups all-purpose flour
> ½ teaspoon salt
> 1 teaspoon baking soda
> 1 cup buttermilk (or see page 85 for alternatives)

Preheat a very hot oven (425°F). Mix the flour, salt and soda together in a bowl, then stir in the buttermilk and mix to a soft dough. Turn onto a floured worktop and knead quickly and lightly. Form the dough into a flat, round cake, about 2 inches high, and cut a deep cross in it to ensure that it cooks evenly. Put on a floured baking sheet and bake in the hot oven for 30–40 minutes or until well risen and lightly browned. When cooked, it will sound hollow when tapped on the base. Cool on a wire rack and eat very fresh with butter and homemade jam.

Makes 1 loaf or 4 triangles.

VARIATIONS

Some people add a little sugar (½–1 teaspoon) with the dry ingredients. A small amount of butter (up to 2 tablespoons) rubbed into the dry ingredients or melted and added with the buttermilk enriches the bread and helps it to keep better.

◆ *Fruit Soda Bread* ◆

This tea bread is very popular in the north of Ireland, so it is especially appropriate to give Florence Irwin's recipe.

> 6 cups all-purpose flour
> 1 teaspoon baking soda
> 1 teaspoon cream of tartar
> ½ teaspoon salt
> 2 tablespoons sugar
> 6 tablespoons butter (optional)
> ⅞ cup currants
> ⅞ cup golden raisins
> 2 ounces mixed peel
> 1½ cups buttermilk

Preheat a very hot oven (425°F). Sift together the dry ingredients. Rub in the butter, if you use it. Add the cleaned fruit and the mixed peel. Mix quickly and lightly with the buttermilk to make a fairly wet dough. Turn the mixture onto a floured board, dredge the dough with flour and knead it lightly. When smooth underneath, turn it upside down and roll out lightly to make a round. Cut a deep cross in the middle to make 4 triangles and place on a floured baking sheet. Bake in the hot oven for 45 minutes or until risen, nicely brown and cooked through. The bread should sound hollow when you tap its base. Cool on a wire rack.

Makes 4 triangles.

——◆ King Sitric Brown Bread ◆——

The King Sitric is a leading seafood restaurant and they have made this bread to great acclaim since the restaurant opened in 1971. It is interesting to note that this recipe seems to have a direct line of descent from the old bastable oven, as it is cooked in a cast-iron casserole with the lid on.

4⅔ cups coarse whole-wheat flour, preferably stoneground
1 cup all-purpose flour
1 rounded teaspoon baking soda
1 teaspoon salt
2 teaspoons sugar
2½ cups buttermilk (or see page 85 for alternatives)
2 tablespoons melted butter

Preheat a very hot oven (425°F). Heat a 1½–2 quart cast-iron casserole with a lid. Mix the flours, soda, salt and sugar in a large bowl, add the buttermilk and mix thoroughly to make a very wet mixture. Mix in the melted butter and turn into the hot casserole, then cover with the lid and bake in the oven for 1 hour, removing the lid for the last 10 minutes to allow the top to brown. Remove from the oven and turn the loaf onto a wire rack; wrap in a damp linen towel and leave to cool.

Makes 1 large loaf.

Whole-Wheat
——◆ Griddle Scones ◆——

If you are ever lucky enough to stay at Roundwood House, Co. Laois, you may well get these scones for breakfast as that's when Rosemarie Kennan serves them, straight from her hotplate. She finds its even temperature much better than modern gas or electric burners for this old family recipe, and she uses an old cast-iron griddle, although a heavy frying pan will do instead.

1 ¼ cups whole-wheat flour
⅓ cup quick-cooking oatmeal
1 level teaspoon baking soda
Pinch of salt
About 7 ounces buttermilk

Have a griddle or heavy frying pan heating on the stove. Mix together the dry ingredients in a bowl, then stir in enough buttermilk to make a very wet consistency. Lightly grease the griddle or pan, or sprinkle it with flour. Put dessert spoonfuls of the mixture onto the hot griddle and cook for 5–6 minutes on each side, until well risen and golden brown. Wrap in a clean linen towel or napkin and serve hot or cold, with butter and homemade jam.

Makes 8 scones.

◆ *Buttermilk Scones* ◆

These lovely light scones are baked in the oven and can be varied to make whole-wheat scones (using half white and half fine whole-wheat flour) or golden raisin scones (by adding ½–⅔ cup golden raisins with the sugar).

4 cups all-purpose flour
½ teaspoon salt
1 teaspoon baking soda
4 tablespoons (½ stick) butter, at room temperature
1 tablespoon granulated sugar
1 small egg, lightly beaten
About 1 cup buttermilk

Preheat a very hot oven (425°F). Grease 2 baking trays. Sift the flour, salt and soda into a bowl. Cut the butter in and rub in until the mixture resembles fine bread crumbs. Add the sugar and mix well. Make a well in the middle and add the lightly beaten egg and enough buttermilk to make a soft dough. Turn onto a floured work surface and knead lightly into shape. Roll out to about ½ inch thick and cut out 12 large or 18 small scones with a fluted cutter, gathering the trimmings and lightly re-rolling as necessary. Arrange on the baking trays, leaving space between. Bake in the hot oven for 15–20 minutes until well risen and golden brown, reversing the position of the trays halfway through. Cool on wire racks and serve very fresh with butter and homemade jam.

Makes about 12 large scones or 18 small ones.

◆ *Oatcakes* ◆

Oatcakes predated other forms of bread in Ireland and were originally baked on flagstone griddles known as bakestones. In her book *The Cookin' Woman* Florence Irwin gives a recipe for what she calls "Modern Oat Cakes," which is very similar to the recipe below (but without the flour, which was a later addition). Her oatcakes were cooked on one side only on a hot griddle, until they dried and curled, then were removed to toast in the oven or under the grill—a modernized version of the traditional process of "harning" in front of the fire. Homemade oatcakes are delicious with plenty of butter and any cheese. They are not hard to make as long as you don't expect them to turn out as neatly as bought ones.

> 8 ounces McCann's Irish Oatmeal, plus extra for the
>   work surface
> ¾ cup all-purpose flour
> Good pinch of baking soda
> Good pinch of salt
> 2 tablespoons bacon fat or butter, melted

Preheat a very hot oven (425°F). Put the dry ingredients into a bowl and mix well. Add the melted bacon fat or butter and blend in thoroughly. Add enough hot water from the kettle to make a spongy mass—don't attempt to make the mixture stiff enough to roll out.

Scatter oatmeal thickly on the work surface, turn the mixture onto it and scatter the top with more oatmeal. Using the backs of the fingers, press the lump out into a round, keeping it dry with oatmeal on top and making sure there is always plenty underneath to prevent it sticking. Continue pressing out in this way until it is thin enough to roll — by now it will have absorbed nearly as much oatmeal as there was in the original ingredients. Make sure there is plenty of oatmeal on the board, then roll out thinly with short, sharp rolls. Before cutting, scatter some fresh oatmeal on top and rub it lightly with the palm of the hand to whiten it. Cut into squares or triangles, lift onto ungreased baking trays and bake in the hot oven for 15 minutes, or until crisp. Cool on a wire rack. When absolutely cold, store in an airtight tin.

Makes about 30 oatcakes.

✦ *Pratie Oaten* ✦

Pratie oaten is a potato oaten cake, also known as "rozel" in Co. Antrim. There are no set quantities for the ingredients — it all depends how much leftover cooked potato you have and how much oatmeal it can absorb. Pratie oaten makes a delicious alternative to potato as a vegetable or side dish and deserves to be more widely used, in the same way as potato galettes.

> Cooked potatoes
> Salt to taste
> McCann's Irish Oatmeal

Mash the potatoes on a work surface, sprinkle with salt and work enough oatmeal into them to form a dough. Sprinkle the work surface with oatmeal and roll the dough out fairly thinly. Cut into triangles, or use a 2–3 inch round cutter to stamp out circles. Bake on a hot griddle or in a heavy frying pan on both sides until golden brown. Best eaten hot with plenty of butter, or fried in bacon fat.

Griddle-Baked
◆ Potato Cakes ◆

This is the older method of making potato cakes, on a griddle or frying pan. Griddle-baked potato cakes were often buttered and eaten hot with sugar, rather like pancakes, while fried ones were cooked in bacon drippings and eaten with bacon slices for breakfast.

> 1 pound freshly cooked potatoes, preferably still warm
> Good pinch of salt
> 2 tablespoons butter, melted
> About 1 cup all-purpose flour

Peel the potatoes and mash them until very smooth. Season with a sprinkling of salt and drizzle the melted butter over. Knead in as much flour as is needed to make a pliable dough — waxy potatoes will need more than naturally floury ones. The mixture should be elastic enough to roll out, but avoid over-kneading as this toughens the dough. Roll out to make a large, fairly thin circle, cut into triangles and bake on a hot griddle or heavy frying pan until brown on both sides.

Makes 4 triangles.

VARIATION

Commercial versions of this are available throughout Ireland as thin, precooked potato cakes that are usually heated through and browned in bacon fat, then served with bacon and eggs for breakfast. Of course, they are much better made from fresh ingredients. If frying the mixture given above, you are making a northern specialty also known as "fadge," which is an indispensable part of the great Ulster Fry, have some hot bacon fat smoking in a heavy frying pan and fry the potato cake in it until brown on both sides. Serve immediately with fried bacon, sausages, eggs and tomatoes for breakfast or high tea.

BOXTY

Boxty is a specialty of the northwestern part of Ireland and, as Padraig Og Gallagher of Gallagher's Boxty House in Dublin put it, "There are as many recipes for boxty as there are parishes in Leitrim." However, at the risk of being deluged with letters of indignation, boxty really falls into three basic groups—boxty bread or cakes ("boxty on the griddle"), boxty pancakes ("boxty on the pan"), and boxty dumplings, which are less well known. Boxty is traditional at Halloween in some areas and it has probably inspired more popular rhymes than any other dish, one of the earliest going back to the days of Bonnie Prince Charlie:

> *I'll have none of your boxty,*
> *I'll have none of your blarney,*
> *But I'll throw my petticoats over my head*
> *And be off with my royal Charlie!*

The traditions similar to those associated with barm brack, such as predicting weddings in the forthcoming year, are more common, however, and the best-known boxty rhyme is undoubtedly:

> *Boxty on the griddle, boxty on the pan,*
> *If you don't eat boxty, you'll never get a man.*

———— • *Boxty Bread, or Boxty on the Griddle* • ————

Boxty bread, or cake, is made in much the same way as potato cake.

> 1 pound potatoes
> 1 pound freshly mashed potatoes
> Salt
> Flour

Peel the potatoes and grate them, using a grater attachment on a food processor, if you have one. Turn them onto a clean linen towel and wring them out tightly, catching all the liquid in a bowl. Leave the liquid until the starch sinks, then pour off the clear water on top. Add both the grated and the mashed potatoes to the starch and mix well. Add salt to taste. Work in just enough flour to make a pliable dough in the same way as for griddle-baked potato cakes (see page 92). Then knead lightly, roll out into a circle and cut into triangles. Bake on a hot griddle or heavy frying pan, like potato cakes, then butter and serve hot. Leftovers are good the next day, sliced, fried in bacon fat and served wtih bacon slices.

Makes 4 triangles.

VARIATIONS
Boxty dumplings are made with the same ingredients as boxty bread but the dough — which sometimes has currants and raisins added to it — is formed into balls about the size of a golf ball after kneading. These are flattened and cooked in lightly salted boiling water for 45 minutes, then drained and served with sweet cornstarch sauce.

◆ *Boxty Pancakes, or Boxty on the Pan* ◆

This version of boxty pancakes is the one that Gallagher's Boxty House is using to such good effect on their traditional Irish menu. They have modernized the way it is served, rather than the recipe itself, and the result is a deliciously light, thin pancake that serves as a container for all sorts of tasty fillings, such as smoked fish, bacon and cabbage with parsley sauce, chicken with leeks, or beef with horseradish. The quantities given below are only a starting point as the recipe is endlessly variable: Adjust the amount of milk and flour depending on how thin you like your pancake. Include cooked mashed potato, but add enough milk so you can drop spoonfuls on a pan.

1 pound potatoes
½–¾ cup all-purpose flour
About ½ cup milk
Salt to taste
A little butter or drippings

Peel and chop the potatoes, then process in a blender or food processor until thoroughly liquidized. Add flour and enough milk to give a dropping consistency. Season to taste with salt. Heat a little butter or dripping on a griddle or cast-iron frying pan. Pour about a quarter of the mixture onto the the pan — if the consistency is correct it will spread evenly over the pan. Cook over moderate heat for about 5 minutes on each side, depending on the thickness of the cake, and serve rolled with a hot filling.

Makes 4 pancakes.

──◆ Buttermilk Pancakes ◆──

With the Lenten Fast about to start the next day, on Ash Wednesday, Shrove Tuesday was a day when "nobody should be without meat." Even in very poor households there was some meat for supper, even if only a little bit of bacon, but it was one of the many occasions when the more prosperous farmers would kill an animal and send parts of it to their poorer neighbors as gifts. Until recently the Lenten Fast was taken so seriously in Ireland that it meant abstaining not only from meat but also eggs and all milk products — a very severe restriction on people whose diet consisted largely of dairy products. So the tradition of making pancakes on Shrove Tuesday originally came about as a practical way of using up surplus eggs, milk and butter that would otherwise go to waste. The rather dubious honor of tossing the first pancake went to the eldest unmarried daughter, whose luck in having "the pick of the boys" depended on tossing it neatly. If she "tossed the cake crooked" (when somebody jogged her elbow, for example!) she had no chance of marrying in the coming year. If successful, she cut the pancake into as many pieces as there were guests and passed them around. Sometimes the mother's wedding ring was slipped into the batter used for the first pancake. The person who got the lucky slice would not only be first married but especially fortunate in her or his choice of husband or wife.

> 4 cups all-purpose flour
> 1 teaspoon baking soda
> 1 teaspoon salt
> Buttermilk
> 4 eggs
> A little drippings

Sift the flour, soda and salt into a large bowl and make a well in the middle. Beat in enough buttermilk with the eggs to make a thick batter. Heat a griddle or heavy frying pan, grease lightly with a little fat and drop spoonfuls of the mixture onto the hot pan. Cook on one side until bubbles rise, then flip over and brown the second side. Serve immediately, sprinkled with sugar, or hot-buttered with honey or homemade jam.

Makes 3–4 dozen pancakes.

BRACKS

The brack is probably the most Irish of all cakes and gets its name from the word *breac*, meaning speckled. There are two basic types of brack, one yeasted and known as barm brack, the other made with baking powder and usually called tea brack because the dried fruit is soaked in cold tea before mixing, but there are countless variations in each category.

Barm brack is now mainly a Halloween specialty, although it has traditionally been associated with a variety of other festivals, notably St. Brigid's Day, February 1 (traditionally the first day of spring in Ireland), and the festival of Luanasa, which began the harvest on August 1 (traditionally the first day of autumn). Tea bracks, which are simpler to make, are more likely to be made throughout the year like other cakes. Symbolic objects intended to divine the future are often included in bracks, notably a ring, a small silver coin, a button, a thimble, a chip of wood and a rag (these days, all hygienically wrapped in foil). The ring signified early marriage, usually within the year, the coin wealth, the button bachelorhood and the thimble spinsterhood. Bleak futures were foretold by the wood, which predicted a stormy marriage, and the rag, which indicated poverty. On the other hand, the most unusual and romantic symbol was a tiny wooden boat, which signified that the recipient would make a journey to the Skellig Rocks and lead a life of single blessedness!

──◆ *Traditional Barm Brack* ◆──

This is Florence Irwin's version of the traditional yeasted brack, and it is of interest to note that she says the name should be *bam* brack. The name is generally supposed to refer to the yeast in the brack but, as the original Irish name is *bairín-breac*, she could well be right. Miss Irwin's recipe is divided into two sections, the first making the yeast "sponge," the second mixing in the remaining ingredients. Instead of making it into large bracks, use the same mixture to make small buns.

First mixture:

> 2 cups all-purpose flour
> 2 tablespoons fresh yeast
> 1 teaspoon sugar
> 1½ cups milk

Heat a bowl, warm the flour and sift it into the bowl. Mix the yeast and sugar in a small bowl. Make the milk just lukewarm (if too hot it will kill the yeast instead of making it grow). Stir this into the yeast. Make a well in the center of the flour. Using a wooden spoon, stir in the yeast mixture to form a batter. Cover the bowl with a towel and a blanket and set to rise in a warm place for 1 hour. Keep the bowl turned if the heat is only to one side of it.

Second mixture:
> 1¾ cups golden or dark raisins
> 4 ounces mixed peel
> ⅞ cup currants
> 5 cups all-purpose flour
> ½ cup sugar
> 8 tablespoons (1 stick) butter
> 2 eggs
> Rings, wrapped in parchment paper
> Sugar to glaze
> Citron peel to garnish

Combine the fruits for the cake. Sift the flour and sugar and rub in the butter. Add the fruit. Beat the eggs. The first mixture, or "sponge," should be thoroughly risen. Place the bowl on the table and, using your hand, work in the second mixture, adding the beaten egg when consistency requires it, as the mixture should never be allowed to become stiff. When well mixed, knead sturdily for at least 5 minutes. Again cover with a towel and a blanket and set to rise for 1½ hours.

To form the barm brack: Divide the dough into 2 or 3 pieces, according to the size required. Have a ring wrapped in parchment paper for each piece. Knead each piece until smooth by turning the edges into the center until smooth underneath. Before turning upside down, stick in a ring. Turn upside down and roll out about 1½ inches thick. Place on a floured baking sheet. Do the others in the same way.

Proof in a warm oven for 30 minutes. Bake in a very hot oven (425°F) for 30 minutes or until cooked.

To glaze: Brush with sugar melted in a little water. Dredge with sugar and place a thin slice of citron peel on the center of each. Return to the oven until dry and glazed, about 2 or 3 minutes. Cool on a wire rack. Serve in slices, freshly buttered.

Makes 2 or 3 bracks.

VARIATION

Most brack recipes include pumpkin pie spice in the ingredients — 1 teaspoon would be about right for these quantities.

⬥ *Tea Brack* ⬥

This unyeasted version of the traditional barm brack is popularly eaten at Halloween instead of the yeasted one and is more often baked at other times of the year also.

> 1¾ cups raisins
> 1¾ cups golden raisins
> ¾ cup dark brown sugar
> 1 cup cold tea
> 4 ounces mixed peel
> Grated rind of 1 orange
> 8 tablespoons (1 stick) butter, melted
> 2 eggs, lightly beaten
> 4 cups all-purpose flour
> 2 level teaspoons baking powder
> 1 teaspoon pumpkin pie spice
> ½ teaspoon cinnamon
> Pinch of salt
> Ring wrapped in parchment paper (optional)
> 1 tablespoon sugar to glaze

Put the raisins, golden raisins and brown sugar in a saucepan with the strained tea. Bring slowly up to boiling point, stirring occasionally, then allow to cool. It can be left overnight if convenient.

Preheat a moderate oven (350°F). Grease a 9-inch round deep cake tin and line the bottom with wax paper. Add the mixed peel and grated orange rind to the mixture along with the melted butter and lightly beaten eggs. Sift the dry ingredients together and gradually stir into the fruit mixture. Stir well, making sure all ingredients are thoroughly mixed together. Add the ring, if using. Turn the mixture into the prepared tin and bake for 1½–2 hours, until the top of the cake feels firm to the touch. Glaze in the same way as the previous recipe. Cool in the tin and serve sliced and buttered.

Makes 1 9-inch round cake.

VARIATION

Use up to ½ cup whiskey to replace some of the tea if desired.

◆ *Irish Apple Cake* ◆

This lovely moist cake is very popular in farmhouse kitchens in the late autumn, when there is an abundance of apples. For the same reason it is often served at Halloween, although it is not associated with Halloween customs in the way that barm brack is. Serve it cold, as a cake, or warm with cream or custard as a pudding.

> 2 cups self-rising flour
> Pinch of salt
> 1 teaspoon ground cloves
> 8 tablespoons (1 stick) butter, at room temperature
> 3–4 cooking apples
> About ¾ cup granulated sugar, or to taste
>   (see method)
> 2 eggs
> A little milk to mix
> Granulated sugar to sprinkle over.

Grease an 8-inch springform cake pan and line the bottom with wax paper. Preheat a fairly hot oven (375°F). Sift the flour, salt and cloves into a bowl, cut in the butter and rub in until the mixture is like fine bread crumbs. Peel and core the apples, slice thinly, and add to the rubbed-in mixture with the sugar — the amount depends on how much sweetening the apples need. Mix in the eggs and enough milk to make a fairly stiff dough, then turn the mixture into the prepared pan and sprinkle with granulated sugar. Bake in the preheated oven for 45 minutes, until crisp, golden brown and springy to the touch.

Makes 1 8-inch cake.

VARIATION

Irish Pear Cake: Substitute pears for the apples. This is a good way to deal with damaged or underripe pears that are unsuitable for use as dessert fruit. If using pears, substitute ground ginger for the cloves.

⸻✦ *Irish Whiskey Cake* ✦⸻

This delicious cake, with its subtle flavors of lemon and cloves, is reminiscent of the famous toddy, hot Irish whiskey.

> 1¾ cups golden raisins
> Grated rind of 1 lemon
> ½ cup whiskey
> 12 tablespoons (1½ sticks) butter, softened
> ¾ cup firmly packed brown sugar
> 3 eggs
> 1½ cups all-purpose flour
> Pinch of salt
> Pinch of ground cloves
> 1 teaspoon baking powder

Icing:

> Juice of 1 lemon
> 1¾ cups confectioners' sugar
> A little warm water
> Crystallized lemon slices to garnish (optional)

Put the raisins and grated lemon rind into a bowl with the whiskey and let soak overnight. Grease a 7-inch-deep cake pan and line the bottom with wax paper. Preheat a moderate oven to 350°F. Cream the butter and sugar until light and fluffy. Separate the eggs. Sift the flour, salt, cloves and baking powder together into a bowl. Beat the yolks into the butter and sugar one at a time, including a spoonful of flour and beating well after each addition. Gradually add the raisins and whiskey mixture, alternating with the remaining flour. Do not overbeat at this stage. Finally, whisk the egg whites until stiff and fold them into the mixture with a metal spoon. Turn into the prepared pan and bake in the preheated oven for about 1½ hours, or until well risen and springy to the touch — test with a skewer, which should come out clean, if you are uncertain. Turn out and cool on a wire rack.

Meanwhile, make the icing by mixing the lemon juice with sifted confectioners' sugar and just enough warm water so that you can pour the icing. Put a dinner plate under the cake rack to catch the drippings and pour the icing over the cake a tablespoonful at a time, letting it dribble naturally down the sides. Don't worry if a lot of it ends up on the plate underneath, just scoop it up and put it on top again. When the icing has set, you can decorate it with crystallized lemon slices, if you like.

Makes 1 7-inch cake.

———— ✦ *Cream Sponge* ✦ ————

This perennial favorite never seems to date and is especially delicious in the summer, filled with the new season's jam. My mother-in-law remembers it having pride of place on the tea table many years ago when she went to visit her aunts, and it is just as popular today. A fatless sponge should be eaten on the day it is made but, in the unlikely event of some being left over, it can be used as a trifle base.

Have all ingredients at warm room temperature for this recipe. Unless you are using a powerful electric mixer, you will need to whisk the eggs and sugar over hot water to get the required volume and consistency.

> 4 eggs
> ½ cup sugar, plus 1 teaspoonful
> 1⅞ cup all-purpose flour, sifted, plus 1 teaspoonful
> Confectioners' sugar for dusting

Filling:
> Raspberry jam
> ⅔ cup heavy cream

Grease an 8-inch-deep cake pan, preferably a springform pan, and dust it with 1 teaspoon of sugar mixed with an equal quantity of flour. Preheat a fairly hot oven (375°F). Put the eggs and sugar into the bowl of an electric mixer and whisk at high speed until the mixture is light and thick and leaves a good trail as it drops from the whisk. If whisking by hand, or with a hand-held electric whisk, set the bowl over a saucepan or another bowl a quarter filled with hot (not boiling) water and whisk until thick and creamy, then remove from the heat. Sift the flour evenly over the whisked eggs and carefully fold it in with a metal spoon, mixing thoroughly, but losing as little volume as possible. Pour the mixture into the prepared tin, level off the top and bake in the preheated oven for 25–30 minutes, until the sponge feels springy to the touch. Let stand for 1–2 minutes to allow the cake to cool a little and shrink slightly from the pan. Then loosen the sides gently with a knife and turn out onto a rack to cool.

When completely cold, slice the sponge across the middle and spread the bottom half generously with homemade raspberry jam. Whip the cream until it forms soft peaks, and use to cover the jam. Put the second half of the cake on top and dust with confectioners' sugar. Leave in the refrigerator for an hour or so, to allow the flavors to blend and the whipped cream to firm up.

Makes 1 8-inch sponge.

VARIATION

Strawberry Gâteau: This cake can very easily be used to make a luscious summer dessert. Omit the jam and double the amount of cream. Hull about 1 pound strawberries. Select some well-shaped, evenly sized ones for the top of the cake and slice the rest. Whip the cream with a little confectioners' sugar so that it is stiff enough to hold its shape. Divide half of it between the two inner sides of the sandwich. Lay the bottom half on a serving plate and arrange the sliced strawberries on the cream. Cover with the second half of the cake and press down gently so that it all holds together. Spread the remaining cream on top of the cake and arrange the reserved strawberries, whole or halved according to size, on top. Set aside for an hour or so for the flavors to develop. Then dust lightly with confectioners' sugar and serve as a dessert the day you make it. This gâteau will serve 8.

⬩ *Boiled Fruit Cake* ⬩

This cake has always been a great favorite in Belfast. It is easy to make and has an unusual texture, different from other fruit cakes.

8 ounces (2 sticks) butter
1 cup plus 2 tablespoons firmly packed brown sugar
1 cup hot water
1¾ cups golden raisins
1¾ cups raisins
1¾ cups currants
4 ounces mixed peel
4 cups all-purpose flour
Pinch of salt
½ level teaspoon baking soda
1 rounded teaspoon pumpkin pie spice
1 teaspoon grated nutmeg
2 eggs

Grease a deep 9-inch round cake pan and line the bottom with wax paper. Put the butter, sugar and water into a saucepan and bring to a boil, stirring until the butter has melted and the sugar has dissolved. Add the dried fruit and mixed peel, bring back up to a boil and simmer over low heat for 3 minutes. Remove from the heat, turn the mixture into a large bowl and let cool until lukewarm.

Meanwhile, preheat a moderately warm oven to 325°F. Sift the flour, salt, soda and spices into a bowl and make a well in the center. Beat the eggs and add to the flour with the cooled fruit mixture. Stir quickly. When thoroughly mixed, turn the mixture into the pre-pared pan and smooth the top. Bake in the preheated oven for 1½–2 hours, until springy to the touch and shrinking slightly from the sides. Test with a skewer if you are unsure — it should come out clean from the center of the cake when it is ready. Cool in the pan; then turn out, remove the base paper and store in an airtight cake tin.

Makes 1 9-inch cake.

Mr. Guinness's Christmas Cake

This cake is quite easy to make and, as it isn't as rich as a traditional Christmas cake and can be used within a week of baking, it is more suitable for making throughout the year. The Guinness adds color and moisture as well as flavor.

> 8 ounces (2 sticks) butter
> 1 cup dark brown sugar
> 4 eggs
> ⅔ cup all-purpose flour
> 2 level teaspoons pumpkin pie spice
> 1¾ cups raisins
> 1¾ cups golden raisins
> 4 ounces mixed peel
> 1 cup walnuts, chopped
> 8–12 tablespoons Guinness

Preheat a moderately warm oven (325°F). Grease a deep 7-inch cake tin and line it with a double layer of greased wax paper. Cream the butter and sugar together until light and creamy. Lightly beat the eggs. Sift the flour and spice together. Gradually beat the eggs into the butter and sugar, adding a little flour and beating well after each addition, then fold in the remaining flour and spice. Add the raisins, golden raisins, mixed peel and chopped walnuts. Mix well and stir in about 4 tablespoons of Guinness to make a soft dropping consistency. Turn into the prepared tin and bake in the preheated oven for 1 hour, then reduce the oven to 300°F, and continue cooking for another 1½ hours, or until a skewer thrust into the center of the cake comes out clean, without any uncooked mixture attached. Let the cake cool in the tin, then turn out and remove the paper. Turn upside down and prick the base of the cake all over with a skewer, then spoon over the remaining 4–8 tablespoons of Guinness. When it has been absorbed, wrap the cake in wax paper and store in an airtight tin for at least a week before using.

Makes 1 7-inch cake.

8. Basic Recipes

STOCK

Fresh stocks are very little trouble, but they make all the difference. There are six basic stocks but, for practical purposes in the home, most needs are covered by a good chicken stock and a fish stock. Vegetables, especially white ones such as onions and celery, contribute a lot to the flavor of stocks, but avoid potatoes as they will make the stock cloudy. Also use strongly flavored root vegetables such as turnips with care, as they may overpower other flavors. Salt is better added at the time of use, depending on other ingredients and the concentration. Vegetable stock can be specially made if required in large quantities (in a vegetarian household, for example) but in most kitchens it is adequate to collect the cooking water from vegetables, keep it in a bottle in the refrigerator and use for gravies, etc., as required.

⬥ *Chicken Stock* ⬥

You can easily adapt this to make a game stock, by using a game bird instead of a chicken. The amount made varies according to the amount of reduction during the long simmering.

> 2 onions
> 1 leek
> 2 carrots
> 2—3 sticks of celery
> Carcass and giblets of 1 chicken
> A few black peppercorns
> Bunch of fresh herbs as available — parsley,
>   thyme, a bay leaf, tied together

Peel, trim and chop roughly the vegetables. Place everything in a large pan, cover generously with 2½—3 quarts water and bring slowly up to the boil. Reduce the heat and simmer gently for 3—4 hours, then strain through a fine sieve. Let cool. When cold, skim any fat off the top. Keep the stock in the refrigerator and use within 3 days, reboiling before use. Alternatively, freeze until required. For use in sauces, hard-boil to reduce the stock to give a concentrated flavor.

⬥ *Fish Stock* ⬥

You can make fish stock quickly. Unlike meat and poultry stocks, which benefit from long simmering to draw out the flavors, fish stock develops a bitter flavor if cooked for a long time. Use any white fish bones and trimmings for a basic stock. Oily fish, such as mackerel or herring, are unsuitable for stock but salmon should only be used to make stock for salmon dishes. Cod and haddock trimmings make the stock cloudy, so avoid them if clarity is important.

> 1½ pounds white fish bones and trimmings
> 3 cups water
> 1 cup dry white wine or cider (optional, but
>   make up with extra water if not using)
> 1 onion, sliced
> 1 carrot, chopped
> 1 stick of celery or 1 leek, sliced
> Broken parsley stalks
> A few black peppercorns, roughly crushed

Put all the ingredients except the peppercorns into a large saucepan and bring to a boil. Reduce the heat and simmer, uncovered, for about 20 minutes, adding the peppercorns for the last 5–10 minutes. Strain through a fine nylon sieve and let cool. Keep in the refrigerator and use within 2 days, otherwise freeze and use as required. Small quantities are often useful—freeze in yogurt cups and ice-cube trays.

Makes about 1 quart.

VARIATION

Court Bouillon: To make a court bouillon used for poaching whole fish or well reduced in sauces, omit the fish bones from the stock but include the wine, plus 2 tablespoons lemon juice or white wine vinegar and a bay leaf. For a richer flavor, increase the proportion of vegetables.

◆ *White Sauce* ◆

The classic white sauce with all its variations is the most generally used in Irish cookery. This recipe is for béchamel, which has a better flavor than the simpler version.

Infusion:

> 1 small onion
> 3 cloves
> 1 bay leaf
>
> 2 cups milk
> 4 tablespoons (½ stick) butter
> ½ cup all-purpose flour
> Sea salt and freshly ground black pepper

First make the infusion: Peel the onion and stud it with the cloves. Rinse out a milk pan with cold water and add the milk, onion and bay leaf. Bring slowly to the boil, then allow to infuse for 15 minutes and strain.

Melt the butter in a saucepan, stir in the flour and cook over low heat for a minute or two, then gradually add the infused milk, stirring all the time to make a smooth sauce. Simmer over low heat for a few minutes, then season to taste. Use as it is as a coating sauce, or thinned to make a pouring sauce, or as a base for any of the following variations:

VARIATIONS

Parsley Sauce: Add 3–4 tablespoons freshly chopped parsley to the finished white sauce and season to taste. If serving with boiled meat, such as bacon, ham or corned beef, replace half the milk with the meat stock. Use fish or vegetable stocks when appropriate.

Cheese Sauce: Add to the finished sauce ½ cup grated sharp Cheddar or other hard cheese, ½ teaspoon prepared mustard and seasoning to taste, including a pinch of cayenne if you like.

Rum, Brandy or Whiskey Sauce: Traditional with Christmas pudding, rum, brandy or whiskey sauce is a variation of white sauce. Make the sauce as above with plain milk and omit all seasonings. Sweeten to taste with about 2 tablespoons sugar and flavor with about ¼ cup rum, brandy or whiskey, or to taste.

◆ Shortcrust Pastry ◆

This general-purpose pastry is most often used for pies, tarts and so on. Keep everything cool when making pastry. Handle as little as possible and chill for 20–30 minutes before rolling.

> 2¼ cups all-purpose flour
> 9 tablespoons butter, or half butter and half lard
> ¼ cup very cold water

Measure the ingredients accurately. Sift the flour into a large bowl, add the butter, and the fat if using, and cut into small pieces. Rub the fat into the flour with fingertips, or using a pastry blender, lifting the mixture as much as possible to aerate. Add the chilled water, mix with a knife or fork until the mixture clings together, then turn onto a floured worktop and knead lightly once or twice until smooth. Wrap in wax paper or foil and leave in the refrigerator to relax for 20 minutes before using.

Enough pastry to line a 9-inch pie pan.

◆ Clarified Butter ◆

Clarified butter has a much higher burning point than ordinary butter and, having had impurities removed, it is excellent for sealing the tops of pâtés and so on. It is expensive for cooking, as 8 ounces of butter makes only about 5 ounces of clarified butter. When you need the real thing, however, this is how to make it:

Melt 8 ounces salted butter in a small pan over gentle heat and cook, without stirring, until the butter begins to foam. Continue, without browning, until the foaming stops. Remove the pan from the heat and let stand until the milky deposits have sunk to the bottom, leaving a clear yellow liquid. Pour this carefully through cheesecloth or muslin into a bowl, leaving all the deposits behind.

◆ *Red Currant Jelly* ◆

Red currant jelly is another indispensable ingredient in a wide range of recipes, quite apart from its value as an accompaniment. Homemade red currant jelly is so superior to the bought variety, which always seems too sweet and flavorless, that it is really worthwhile making it, even if you have to buy the red currants. As red currants are particularly rich in pectin, the fruit can be boiled a second time to produce more juice.

> 3 pounds red currants
> 3 cups water
> 1–1½ cups sugar per cup juice (see method)

Simmer the fruit with 2 cups of the water for 20 minutes, or until the fruit is reduced to a pulp, then strain it through a jelly bag for only 15 minutes. Return the fruit pulp to the pan with the remaining water and simmer for 30 minutes. Strain and allow to drip for 1 hour. Mix the two batches of juice together, measure and allow 1–1½ cups sugar per cup juice (the larger amount is possible because of the high pectin content of the fruit; more sugar gives a higher yield — and, of course, a sweeter jelly). Return the juice to the rinsed pan, add the sugar and stir over gentle heat to dissolve. Bring to the boil, then boil hard for 5–10 minutes, or until setting point is reached. Put quickly into small warmed jars, then cover.

The yield is impossible to guess with any accuracy, but is probably around 4 pounds.

◆ *Irish Whiskey Marmalade* ◆

Whiskey has been predictably popular in homemade marmalade in Ireland — so much so, in fact, that several commercial brands are now available. As anyone who makes his own marmalade will agree, however, even the best of bought ones cannot compare with real homemade marmalade. If the whiskey is added to the hot marmalade before potting, much of the flavor will be lost by evaporation. The way around this is to put a tablespoon or two into each jar before adding the marmalade, so it won't evaporate and the full flavor will develop during storage.

> 3 pounds Seville oranges
> Juice of 2 large lemons
> 3 quarts water
> 6 pounds granulated sugar
> About 1 cup Irish whiskey

Scrub the oranges and pick off the disc at the stalk end. Halve them and squeeze the juice, retaining the seeds. Quarter the peel, cut away any thick white pith and shred the peel as thickly or thinly as you like it. Roughly cut the pith and tie it up with the seeds in a square of muslin or cheesecloth. Tie loosely, so that water can circulate in the bag during cooking and extract the pectin from the pith and seeds; hang from the handle of the preserving pan on a long string. Add the peel, strained orange and lemon juices and the water to the pan. Bring to the boil and simmer for 1½–2 hours or until the peel is quite tender.

Remove the bag of pith and seeds and squeeze it out well between two plates to extract as much pectin as possible. Add the sugar to the pan and stir over low heat until completely dissolved. Bring to the boil, then boil hard for 15–20 minutes or until setting point is reached. Skim, if necessary, and let cool for about 15 minutes, then stir to redistribute the peel. Divide the whiskey between 8–10 warm jam jars and, using a small Pyrex jug, pour in the hot marmalade. Cover and seal while still hot.

Makes 8–10 pounds.

———————— ✦ *Porridge* ✦ ————————

Porridge is a basic dish eaten every day in winter in most Irish households. I make it overnight in an electric slow cooker, using 1 cup porridge oats to 3 cups cold water and a sprinkling of salt. This is the traditional method.

> 1 quart water
> 1 cup McCann's Irish Oatmeal
> Good pinch of salt

Put all the ingredients into a saucepan and bring to the boil, stirring. When the porridge is smooth and begins to thicken, reduce the heat to a simmer and cook gently for 25 minutes, stirring occasionally.

Makes 4 generous servings.

⬩ *Mushroom Ketchup* ⬩

This traditional country relish has always been very popular in Ireland. Until recently butter was a luxury, even to the farmers who made it, so flavorings like this were often used to add interest to boiled potatoes. Nowadays, it is more likely to be used sparingly with chicken and fish dishes and to add flavor to soups and casseroles. Big, flat field mushrooms should be used for their flavor and color. This is Florence Irwin's version:

Preparation: Break the mushrooms and slice the stalks. Put into a crock with a light layer of salt on each layer of mushrooms — about 2 teaspoons salt to 1 pound mushrooms. Leave in a cool place for 3 days, stirring daily.

To extract the juice: Put all into the preserving pan and boil for 5 minutes. Pour into a jelly bag and squeeze out every drop of juice.

To spice: Measure the liquid into an enamelled pot and to every quart allow ¼ ounce whole ginger, 1 teaspoon whole allspice, 3 blades mace, 4 cayenne pods, 4 cloves, 1 teaspoon peppercorns, 1-inch cinnamon stick. Bruise all of these and put in the pot with the liquor. Boil until reduced by half. Skim. Strain through a muslin bag without squeezing. Bottle and cork when cold.

NOTE: The spices may be used for a second boiling with only a few fresh ones added.

9. Beverages

Milk and buttermilk have always been the great traditional Irish country drinks, taken at any time of the day or night and with any meal, but tea became popular during the nineteenth century and is now the most usual everyday drink throughout the country. Various herb teas — dandelion, camomile and so on — were widely made too but, unlike the French who enjoy drinking them, the Irish usually reserved them for medicinal purposes. Beer and cider were commonly made on farms, especially for the Harvest Home, weddings and wakes, and commercially made beer and stout became well known worldwide, of course. Porter was the plain man's drink and Porter Meal may be the origin of the "eatin' and drinkin'" reputation attached to that drink: Peddlers, carters and other traveling people used to carry with them a little bag of oaten meal and when they came to an inn they would buy a glass of porter, mix it with the meal in a bowl and eat it like porridge.

Whiskey was — and still is — another of the great Irish drinks, of course. At Port Ballintrae in Co. Antrim it is an essential ingredient of the event of the year, known locally as "The Salmon Dinner." The menu consists of fish soup, freshly caught salmon, new potatoes and Bushmills whiskey!

In the eighteenth century particularly, brandy and claret were very popular with the gentry, and journals of the time are rich with anecdotes relating to them both.

The other traditional Irish drink that deserves special mention is poteen or poitín, a spirit made from malted barley which has been made secretly in hidden stills deep in rural Ireland since the early seventeenth century, when taxation literally drove production underground. The stills are of varying degrees of sophistication and the end result, a strong, colorless spirit, also varies dramatically in quality. Making poitín is still an illegal activity, but maybe that's half the fun of it. It's still available, anyway, if you know where to get it, and many a respected pillar of society takes pride in knowing where to get "a drop of the good stuff."

◆ Hot Claret ◆

The origin of this hot wine cup goes back to the time when claret was very plentiful — and probably not especially good.

> 1 bottle red claret wine
> 1 cup water
> ¾ cup sugar (or to taste)
> 1 lemon
> 2-inch cinnamon stick

Put the wine, water and sugar into a pan. Thinly peel the lemon with a vegetable peeler and add to the pan along with the cinnamon. Slowly heat, stirring to dissolve the sugar, until almost boiling. Take off the heat, cover and let infuse for 10 minutes. Strain into a heated jug and pour into warmed glasses, each garnished with half a slice of lemon, if you like.

Makes about 10 glasses.

Hot Whiskey or ◆ *Whiskey Punch* ◆

This traditional "cure" for colds is more often drunk simply to counter the effects of the Irish weather. It makes a very enjoyable way to round off a day's winter sporting activities or just a bracing walk.

> 2½ ounces Irish whiskey
> 1 thick slice of lemon, halved
> Whole cloves, to taste
> 1–2 teaspoons crystallized brown sugar to taste

Put the whiskey, lemon slices stuck with cloves and the sugar into a large, stemmed glass or one with a handle. Place a spoon in the glass so the hot water won't break it, then fill up with boiling water. Stir well to dissolve the sugar and drink hot.

Makes 1 drink.

◆ *Gaelic Coffee* ◆

Probably one of Ireland's most famous exports, a good Gaelic coffee is an exercise in contrast and a rare treat indeed. It is really more of a dessert than a drink.

> 1 measure of Irish whiskey
> Strong black coffee
> Crystallized brown sugar to taste
> Lightly whipped heavy cream

Measure the whiskey into a stemmed glass, or one with a handle. Place a spoon in the glass so the hot coffee won't break it and pour in enough freshly made strong black coffee to come to about ½ inch from the top. Sweeten to taste and stir vigorously to dissolve the sugar and create a miniature whirlpool in the glass. Top up with cream, poured down the back of a teaspoon. It will settle to make a distinct layer in creamy contrast to the dark coffee underneath. It is important that the coffee should be very hot to contrast with the cold cream.

Makes 1 drink.

◆ *Blas Meala* ◆

This drink is even more traditional — and even more like a dessert — than Gaelic coffee. Question: do you drink it or eat it with a spoon?

> ½ glass freshly squeezed orange juice
> 1 teaspoon honey
> 1 measure of Irish whiskey
> Lightly whipped heavy cream
> Toasted oatmeal

Heat the orange juice to just below boiling point, add the honey and stir. Pour into a glass, add the whiskey and top with a layer of whipped cream. Sprinkle with freshly toasted oatmeal and drink as quickly as possible.

Makes 1 drink.

◆ *Black Velvet* ◆

There is always controversy over this dashing drink: Is the combination a stroke of genius, or is it a waste of two ingredients that are superb served individually? There is only one way to find out — try it.

> 1 bottle champagne, chilled
> Guinness

Mix the champagne with an equal quantity of Guinness, or to taste, in tall glasses. Drink immediately, while very bubbly.

Makes 10 servings.

⸺ ✦ *Acknowledgments* ✦ ⸺

Thanks are due to the following for kind permission to reprint copyright material: Gill and Macmillan for the extract from *The Ballymaloe Cookbook* by Myrtle Allen; The Mercier Press for extracts from *The Year in Ireland* and *The Hearth and Stall and All* by Kevin Danaher; Pan Books for extracts from *A Taste of Ireland* by Theodora FitzGibbon; Routledge for extracts from *Irish Folk Ways* by E. Estyn Evans. Florence Irwin's recipes are taken from *The Cookin' Woman* (new edition, Blackstaff Press, 1986) and are reproduced by kind permission of the estate of Florence Irwin. Whilst all attempts have been made to find copyright holders of quoted passages, any who feel they have not been acknowledged should contact the author, care of the publisher.

Working on this book has been a rewarding experience and warm thanks are due to the many people who helped me along the way. I am especially grateful to Janet Martin, who gave me my first cookery column in the *Irish Independent* in 1974 and set me firmly on the right road, and to my parents-in-law, who have always been enormously supportive. Special thanks to my mother-in-law for the gift of her copy of Florence Irwin's *The Cookin' Woman*, which has been such a great source of inspiration and pleasure. Thanks also to the many people in restaurants and country houses who were so generous with their time (and their recipes) and to friends and colleagues — particularly Georgina O'Sullivan of The Meat Centre at CBF (Irish Livestock and Meat Board) and Paula Daly of McDonnells Good Food Kitchen — who helped with reminiscences, advice and recipes. Special thanks must also go, of course, to Myrtle Allen and Theodora FitzGibbon for their pioneering work in raising the standard of food in Ireland over the last twenty years: without them, and others like them, there would be no good food from Ireland! On the home front, thanks to my stepdaughter Patricia for her help and encouragement, and to my husband William and our Trainee Tasting Team (Brian, Bobby and David) for tolerating domestic chaos while work was in progress — and for their willingness to eat some very odd meals to help with recipe testing!

On the production side, thanks to Dave Smith, of Dave's Disk

Doctor Service Ltd. in Kent, who salvages corrupted floppy disks for the charity Bacup (the British Association of Cancer United Patients) and rescued me (and a significant portion of the book) from the perils of modern technology! Finally, a very special thank-you to my editor, Jane Middleton — without whom this book would not have been written — for her unstinting encouragement, help and patience throughout the project.

About the Author

Georgina Campbell is a freelance food writer based in Ireland. She has a weekly column in *The Sunday Press*, which is published in Dublin, and contributes to a number of other publications, including *Taste* magazine. She has presented cookery on television, most recently on the BBC series "Catch Of The Day." She lives in a fishing port near Dublin, with her husband and three teenage sons.

Index